TRAMPIN' IN, PARD?

TRAMPIN' IN, PARD?

Of Nevada Miners Then and Now

By
Karen Wilkes

Copyright © 2017 by Karen E. Wilkes

All rights reserved, including the right to reproduce this book or portions thereof in any form whatsoever.

Publisher: Karen E. Wilkes
Nevada@dmartnevada.com
Cover and design by Darryl Martin

Also by Karen Wilkes:

> *Blue Sky and a Buick*
> *Bishop on Horseback*

ISBN 978-0-692-92137-1

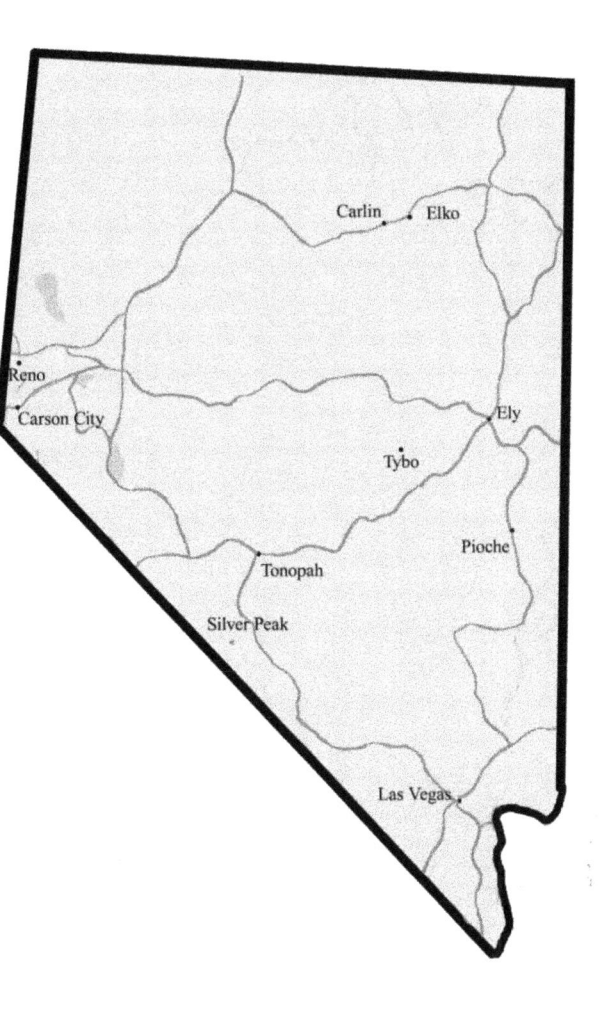

Foreword

Nevada history is a sweeping tale of bonanza and borrasca, of sudden riches and blow sand in almost equal measure.

To understand the state's rise in the general consciousness, you must appreciate its inextricable link with mining and prospecting. Stories of the Comstock Lode and the strikes at Tonopah and Goldfield are truly part of American lore and made a few men almost unfathomably rich. They are chapters filled with as much business and political intrigue as scratching in the ground and boring hundreds of feet beneath the surface.

But to truly appreciate the Silver State, it's essential to understand the miners themselves. Not the promoters, speculators and money men who controlled the mines, but the men who put their backs and their lives into the labor. Most of their names and stories are lost to time.

That's part of what makes Karen Wilkes' "Trampin' In, Pard? Of Nevada Miners Then and Now" such a gemstone. It captures the stories of real Nevada miners, their dreams and disappointments. Reading it, you'll begin to get a sense of the difficult lives of the itinerant miners chased not only fleeting dreams but the work itself from one boomtown to the next.

One part family history, one part memoir, with a lot of thorough research and reporting poured in, "Trampin' In, Pard?" is a fascinating study that brought back memories of some of the stories my father and grandfather told at the end of the day after working the family mining claims in the Old Ivanpah district near the Nevada-California state line a few miles from Interstate 15. Grandpa Curtis had worked on

Boulder Dam and been an ironworker on the construction of the transmission lines that stretched across the desert to Los Angeles. It was during that construction that his crew crossed a part of the high desert near Clark Mountain that intrigued him and sparked a dream of riches.

My dad provided most of the labor. He was raised near Death Valley and worked in a mining mill at twelve years old. He was a construction painter by trade, and a father with a family of six to feed, but he also dreamed of striking it rich and in those years and would drill and blast and muck out silver and tungsten and fluorspar claims for hour after hour.

The family never got rich, of course, but the stories of the fascinating geology of the region, the characters who promoted more than they dug, and the plain folks who possessed the courage to try their own luck filled endless hours by the wood stove.

I learned back then, and am reminded once more after reading Karen Wilkes' wonderful book, that the real stories of Nevada mining aren't in the hills, but in the hearts of those who grabbed pick and shovel, toiled for wages and chased a dream from Searchlight to Pioche and all the way down south to Chile.

John L. Smith is a longtime Nevada journalist and author. In 2016, he was inducted into the Nevada Newspaper Hall of Fame.

For Dysen, Theodore and Rutherford

Introduction

After writing "Blue Sky and a Buick" in 2012 and "Bishop on Horseback" in 2013, the biographies of two Religious leaders, I felt that I needed to take a break from writing and was wondering if I really even had anything else to say. My father, Roscoe Wilkes, was still living at that time and had suggested that I write about the owners of the various mines in Pioche, Nevada, an infamous Nevada mining camp, and our home town.

I gave this subject considerable thought, but just couldn't develop the enthusiasm needed for the hard work that would be involved. However, this contemplation led me to the question, "why has there been so much written about the mines in Nevada and so little written about the thousands of miners who toiled inside these horrible black holes, losing fingers, limbs, the use of their lungs, their hearing, and some losing their lives?" My grandfather, who died long before I was born, was one of these miners, and I had always been fascinated by his life story.

Then, the tragedy surrounding the untimely death of Jack Brown (1953) in the Caselton mine came flooding back to me and reduced me to tears. It quickly became obvious to me that I had to start writing again, and that I had to tell the story of Jack Brown. Pioche is a remote area, and it was very unlikely that anyone else would be writing his story. Jack's widow was deceased, as were most of his fellow miners, and his children were babies when he died – they had no memories of him.

Once I started to chart the layout of a book, I realized, however, that the story of Jack Brown would not be long enough for a book. It quickly came to me that I needed to write the biographies of four miners representing four different eras. I don't know where this idea came from, but once it landed in my head, I was totally committed to this configuration, to the exclusion of all other plans. I felt that I could, hopefully, present a retrospective of mining in Nevada over a period of 100 years through the eyes of these four miners. Then, how to chose the miners?" I wondered. All I can say was that it just happened, and it happened very quickly. When each one was decided upon, I felt immediately calm about the decision – I never wavered from these four men. My husband would ask me, "How do you know that you have the right miner for the story?" I would readily reply, "I just know. He is my miner."

The miners chosen for this book are each very different one from another in personality, motive, and execution; but they all four have had distinguished mining careers in varying ways. Most importantly, all four are "stand-up" kind of guys who have given their all to their careers and have tried to be the best miners that they could be. You will like these miners.

I introduce to you, Jack Brown, ace miner of the No.1 and Caselton mines in Pioche during the 1940's boom and into the 1950's. I would like to introduce Roscoe Hamilton Wilkes, my grandfather, who mined all over the West, northern Mexico, and Chile, making his final stops in Pioche and Tybo, Nevada in 1928.

Meet Paul Barnes, Jr., a man who has prospected for lithium salts in Searles Lake, California and Clayton Valley (Silver Peak) Nevada since the early 1980's, and who has been actively engaged up to this date in legal warfare with the BLM and numerous behemoth mining corporations, fighting for his rights to the potassium tailings at Silver Peak. (Yes, this too is part of being a miner.)

Lastly, I would like to introduce Jordan Hale, a member of Nevada's elite team of gold miners who is mining the Carlin Trend in northeastern Nevada. Jordan comes from a long line of Pioche miners and represents the miners of today and of our future in Nevada.

I am hoping that these four miners will become your close friends, and that by the end of the book you will feel like you, too, have been a Nevada miner, and that you have gained a deeper understanding and love for this great State, Nevada, by engaging in a part of its history.

FOREWORD 1
INTRODUCTION 7
JACK BROWN 13

    SIRENS 15
    JACK AND HAROLD – ON THE ROAD 17
    JOHN CLAYTON KELLY BECOMES JACK BROWN 21
    THE TRAMP MINER CIRCUIT 25
    WELCOME TO NEVADA.. 29
    MINERS RUSH TO PIOCHE 31
    THE STARS ALIGN FOR JACK AND VIRGINIA 37
    LIFE AT THE PIOCHE HOTEL... 39
    COMBINED METALS NO.1 MINE 45
    NO ONE COULD OUT-PRODUCE JACK BROWN 49
    BLACK SLIME – THE WILD CARD 55

WIDOW'S LAMENT 63
ROSCOE HAMILTON WILKES 65

    ROSCOE WRITES HOME 67
    OH GRANDMA! (EARLY 1960'S) 69
    THE MISSING GRANDPA 71
    GRANDPA BECOMES A TRAMP MINER 77
    EL TENIENTE MINE, CHILE 83
    ROSCOE SR. BECOMES A FAMILY MAN 87
    TRAMP MINING WITH BABIES 91
    COASTING INTO PIOCHE 97
    EVERYONE WAS POOR 101
    FOLLOWING GRANDPA'S STEPS TO CHILE 105

PARIS 113
PAUL T. BARNES, JR. 115

    LIFE ON THE "A" LIST... 117
    MEET THE PARENTS 121
    SALTS & DEMONS 125
    THE MAKING OF A MINER 129
    WHAT IS LITHIUM, ANYWAY? 133
    THE BRINE THICKENS 137

    Leprechaun Mining and Mineral Co. 143
    Clyde Passes the Baton to Paul Jr. 149
    Permits and Potassium Go Missing 153
    David Versus Goliath 161

QUOTE 167
JORDAN HALE 169

    The Silver State Turns to Gold 171
    Jordan Finds His Passion 177
    Rubber Tire Mining 181
    Mining in 1936 by Roscoe Wilkes, Jr. 185
    Jordan Mines "Gyppo" 191
    The Miner Takes a Wife 195
    Brassing Out 197

ACKNOWLEDGMENTS 207
BIBLIOGRAPHY 209
GLOSSARY OF MINING TERMS 211

JACK BROWN

Nevada Miner

Sirens

UHRRRUUUAH! UHRRUUUAH! UHRRRRRUUUUUUAHHH!

The sound was deafening – over and over the sirens screeched – "Uhruuuah!"

"*Bobbi Jo, what's going on? Why are the sirens going off like this?*"

"*Don't you know? It means there is a cave-in at the mine, and men are hurt or dead.*"

"*No!*" I didn't know – I didn't know. I stood frozen in one spot, unable to move. I knew what mines were, and I understood that the ground could cave in, but I didn't know that men in my town could be injured or killed. No, I didn't know. I didn't know that a working mine could cave in while men were down inside the mine. I didn't know that a mine could cave in on a daddy with three kids at home.

I was seven years old, and no one had ever told me that men could be killed in a mine. Dear Lord, I didn't know.

"*Bobbi, who is hurt?*"

"*It's the Brown's dad…. Mr. Brown is dead.*"

I knew the Brown kids. There were three children in the Brown family: Dottie, Tommy and the baby, Dawna. How could a mine cave in on a daddy with three kids? How could that happen? I was an only child; there was only one of me and three of them. Why not my daddy instead of theirs? All of the existential questions of the universe came flooding into my seven year old brain in one single moment, and I knew that day that there would never be any easy answers to the hard questions of life.

A deep gut-wrenching sob started to develop in my throat, but I was not at home. I was playing with Bobbi Jo in her neighborhood. I couldn't cry because I was a big girl now. So, I stuffed the deep sob down into the core of my gut; and as time went by, I condensed the sob into a small tight package where it remained until today.

Sixty years later, I am compelled to share the story of my people, the miners of Nevada, and of the world in which they live.

Jack and Harold – On the Road

"Alone from night to night you'll find me.
Too weak to break the chains that bind me.
I need no shackles to remind me.
I'm just a prisoner of love......,"

Jack Brown grips the wheel with both hands, as he croons with all the needed emphasis to convince himself that he is just as good a singer as Perry Como— and as handsome too, for that matter.

It's 4 o'clock in the afternoon – the sun, a big yellow globe, slowly descends toward the desert floor, coloring the clay dirt flaming orange for miles in all directions and the gray mountains various shades of purple – the vista becoming a grand display of carnival glass.

"Ya know, Jack, I really think you need to break outta those chains and find a new song," drawls Harold.

"Ha – You're just jealous of my fine voice and Sinatra phrasing," chuckles Jack.

"Uh huh – Well should we pull over in Holbrook or keep driving to Winslow? I'm startin' to thirst for a cold Bud."

"That's the best idea you've had all day, pard. Ya know, I'm still thinkin' about the look on that shift boss' ugly snout when I told him I

was leavin' at the end of the shift. 'Why,' he says, 'aint this huge copper outfit good enough for ya?'"

"And, I said, 'Well, pard, you might try treatin' your men with the due respect that they deserve, along with maybe replacing some of this World War I equipment that's fallin' apart; and maybe, just maybe, some of these fine miners would stick around.' Then he said, 'Well I guess your buddy on night shift will be trampin' out too?'"

"And so I told him, 'I don't speak for my buddy, and my buddy don't speak for me.'" Jack laughs and hits the steering wheel with his right hand. "I wasn't about to cheat you out of an opportunity to take your own shot at that old, rough-as-a-cob bastard. Good riddance!"

Harold chuckles and says, "Yeah – I'm ready for a new mine, a new foreman, a new shift boss, and tonight a clean bed and a great big steak. Let's stop at Winslow. Who knows, there might be a poker game somewhere, or they might have a picture show.

"And, even better yet, there might be a couple of dolls on their way to L.A., just gettin' off the train for the night; and they just might be lookin' for a couple of rich, handsome miners."

"Well, you got the handsome right," Harold observes.

Jack Brown and Harold Goodman were joined at the hip and had been from age nine or ten. Their parents had been friends in southeast Arizona when they were young children. Harold's mother, Quinnie Pearl, had given birth to Harold on Feb. 1, 1923, when she was sixteen. She divorced Harold's father when Harold was two, and had married Jack Brown's uncle, Buster Brown, which made Jack and Harold cousins by marriage, and was the beginning of a life-long friendship.

As Quinnie, a LPN, moved forward in her career, acquiring and dismissing several other husbands, Harold was left to be raised by his grandmother. By age nine or ten, he was spending more and more time with the Frank Brown family, eventually moving in with them for his high school years—a testament to the large hearts of Nina and Frank Brown, as they had four children of their own and were living solely on Frank's income as a miner.

When World War II broke out, Jack and Harold—now bonded like full brothers— wanted to join the Navy together. Harold was under age 18 and needed a parent's signature to enlist, and Quinnie Pearl was by now residing in another state, making it difficult to obtain her signature.

Either Nina Brown, Jack's mother, came up with a solution, or the two boys came up with the solution and talked Nina into it. Whichever happened, the upshot was that Nina Brown adopted Harold, becoming his legal mother; signed the induction papers for the Navy, and Harold Goodman was now a Navy man.

Jack and Harold were both honorably discharged in 1946, and were anxious after serving four years in the Navy to get back in touch. These two young men were perfect specimens of everything the United States of America had to offer post World War II. They had experienced farm and mining life in the barren deserts of southern Arizona; they had survived the depression in an area of the country offering sparse bounty; they had weathered the boredom of small towns with small schools lacking in resources; and they had both lost their biological fathers.

Jack and Harold were hard workers. They were physically fit, straight thinkers and had good basic values. They brought all of these natural attributes to the Navy along with thousands of other young men just like them, enabling the United States to win a great war. They were fully-functioning, strong men with much to offer any employer in the booming post war economy.

It was not that Jack and Harold would ever be disloyal to an employer; it was just that they had arrived at the place in their lives where they understood their worth. They had survived the War, served their four years for Uncle Sam, and now it was time to have a little fun and see the West, knowing full well that they could get a job any time they wanted in construction or mining, and that seniority was just not a priority at this particular time.

It was the "Jack and Harold" show. They were off to see the West, and the plan was to work an undetermined time at each stop – that is, they would stay on a job as long as it was rewarding; but would definitely leave and move on if the spirit moved them— and that meant they might leave at the end of any shift, or maybe in the middle of the shift, if the situation warranted it. The economy was booming; there were many government construction projects all over the West, and the mines were still operating at wartime production standards. Man-power was in sharp demand, and a couple of young Navy veterans would be hired on the spot at most any jobsite.

As the culture of the mining industry is a bit different from almost any other industry, it was not seen as a detriment to leave a mining job without giving notice. Somehow this culture developed during the early gold rush years in California and Nevada, when men were flooding in to areas of the latest discoveries and then leaving in a flash as soon as the ore veins petered out.

Also, mining is such a dangerous and demanding job that no one ever faulted a miner for not wanting to go at it again the next day. Thus, the terms "trampin' in" and "trampin' out" entered the lexicon of mining terms in the 1800's, and those terms are still used today. Jack and Harold knew this about mining, as they had grown up in southeastern Arizona where there were many mines – copper, gold and silver, and Jack's step-dad, Frank Brown, had mined when Jack was growing up. Our young men were now truly "tramp" miners, feeling their oats and enjoying their new found freedom.

John Clayton Kelly Becomes Jack Brown

John Clayton Kelly, "Jack," was born August 14, 1921, in Douglas, Az., to Hugh Clayton Kelly and Nina Edalene Stone. Hugh came from a ranching family in Ozona, Texas, and Nina was raised on the "N Bar S" ranch near Roswell, New Mexico. The young couple were ranching near Douglas, Arizona, when one day Hugh, riding one horse and leading two others on his way back to the ranch, was struck by lightning, which killed him instantly. It was Aug. 7, 1922, and Jack was just one year old. Nina, Jack's mother, was pregnant when the accident occurred and gave birth to a baby girl, Dorothy, two months after the death of her husband.

These were hard times for Nina, a young woman left alone on a ranch with a toddler and a newborn baby. Hugh Kelly's parents gave Nina all of the emotional support that they could and probably financial support as well. But baby Jack, the eldest child of their deceased son, had become the ardent passion of the Senior Kelly's, which resulted in them feeling it would be best for Nina to give her child to them to raise. Nina would have none of this, resulting in friction between her and the senior Kellys.

To her credit, Nina continued to get by on her own and did not give up her children. On April 22, 1925, she married Frank Brown in Tombstone, Az. They had two more children, William Franklin, born in 1926, and Richard James born in 1930. Unfortunately, the conflict with the senior Kelly's continued, resulting in an unfortunate rift between the children and their grandparents which never healed.

Frank Brown was a wonderful husband and father, who treated all four children as his own. Jack and Dorothy called him "daddy Frank," and he would be the only father they ever knew. Frank Brown did not formally adopt Nina's two children, but they were known as the Brown children in school and socially in town. Nina and her children had landed well.

Frank had a small ranch near Douglas, and in the 1920's he had invested in goats to be raised for mohair. This was a great plan, but the depression came along, the bottom fell out of the mohair market, and the Brown's lost everything along with most everyone else in the United States. He and Nina, shortly after their marriage, sold the ranch at a break-even price and relocated to Bowie, Arizona where Frank worked construction and mined.

Bowie was a great place to raise a family in the 20's and 30's. Jack played various sports and loved all of the opportunities for hunting and fishing. According to his sister, Dorothy, Jack was popular as a child and also as a teenager— well liked by the boys as well as the girls. He graduated from Bowie High School in 1939, a "three letter man". His sister does not remember what Jack did between high school and enlisting in the Navy, but believes that he probably worked construction on one of the dams being built in southern Arizona at that time.

Jack Brown enlisted in the Navy on Sept. 11, 1942, in Phoenix, Arizona. Japan had attacked Pearl Harbor on Dec. 7, 1941, and World War II was in full swing. The enlistment document shows that Jack was living in Safford at the time of his enlistment and was assigned Corpus Christi, Texas as his Duty station. It was at this time that Jack officially changed his name from John Clayton Kelly to John Clayton Brown, as he had been known most of his life.

Jack served as a fireman first class aboard the USS Valeria in 1945. The Valeria was an Artemis Class Attack cargo ship operating in the Asian-Pacific theatre. The ship was launched from Boston Harbor in May of 1945, en route to Hawaii via the Panama Canal. On the way to Oahu, the hostilities in the Pacific ended, and the USS Valeria continued transporting returning troops to the States for the remainder of 1945. Jack was honorably discharged at San Pedro, California on March 10, 1946.

We know that Harold's Duty Station was also Corpus Christie, and that he was serving in Guam when he mustered out. His daughter, Becky Goodman, remembers her dad saying that he left the service six months after Jack, and that they were both very anxious to re-connect and plan the next phase of their civilian lives.

The Tramp Miner Circuit

There are 1,439 documented mines in Arizona, 171 of which are active today. Utah has recorded 702 mines—131 of them active. Montana wins the contest with a total of 3,350 recorded mines—74 active. You can download GPS directions to 643 mines in Idaho. And in 2014, the Nevada mining association documented 24 active metal mines, 24 industrial mineral mines, 6 oil fields and 12 geothermal power plants. However, the total number of recorded mining claims in Nevada is a whopping 4,437. Therefore, if a person held a mining claim anywhere in Nevada, the chances of it being a producing mine today are .0148%— not good odds in a gamblin' State. But, post World War II, there were many profitable working mines all over the West, due to the demand for a variety of metals needed for military equipment and munitions.

We know that Jack Brown and Harold Goodman left southern Arizona some time after being discharged from the Navy in the spring of 1946; but, where did they go from there? According to Harold's step-daughter, Becky Goodman, her father told her that the two guys wanted to see the West and knew that they could easily get construction or mining jobs in many places. She believes they may have worked on the Parker Dam in Arizona first. Perhaps, they might have headed north towards the Utah and Nevada mines, possibly going through Las Vegas on the way, as Harold told Becky that they were both enamored at the time with casinos!

In fact, according to Harold, Jack really liked poker, as well as the casino games, and would at times find himself a big winner. But occasionally, Jack would run into a streak of very bad luck and would find himself on his last dime. Harold came up with the idea of asking Jack for a personal loan when he was "in the chips." Later, when he ran into bad luck, Harold would graciously offer to repay the loan. This system worked very well for Jack, and Harold liked being a part of the solution – great partnership, indeed!

Utah's largest mine during the 1940's, was "Bingham Canyon Mine" near West Jordan, Utah. In Montana, the "AMC" mine in Butte had profited hugely from the war and had become what is now known as the "Anaconda Corporation." Both of these mines would have been large employers and likely targets for our young miners. Also, the largest lead-silver mine in the U.S. today is the "Bunker Hill" mine in the Coeur d'Alene mining district of Idaho, which might have been another likely stopping place.

Jack Brown and Harold Goodman had not invented something new. The traveling miner who called his own career shots had existed in the United States since the gold rush. Darell Free, a Lincoln County, Nevada miner of the 1930's, reports in his oral history:

> *"Well, miners have a different lifestyle than most people. Some miners would go from here to Tybo to Grass Valley to Coeur d'Alene and come back to Butte. They'd make that circle every year. And they never rustled a job. They just came, put on their diggers and went down the hole....They might last only 10 days, or 3 or 4 months."*

Jack and Harold were true "tramp" miners, as of the days of old. We can imagine that they knew tramp miners from their days working in the Arizona mines, and that they had become acquainted with the usual 1940's tramp miner circuits. I suspect that they were not traveling as aimlessly as it first seemed, but driving and/or hitch-hiking to a predetermined number of mines based on information gleaned at each stop along the way. i.e. *"Where are they hiring? What are they paying? What is management like? How is it down in the hole? How far is the mine from the nearest town?"*

    We can, however, rest assured that this duo, Jack and Harold, were having a "once in a life-time," great adventure. Jack was 25 years old, handsome, a skilled miner, a good dancer, and he was traveling with his best friend/adopted brother who was equally handsome and skilled. It doesn't get much better than that. Or, does it?
    Next stop was Pioche, Nevada. According to Becky Goodman, her grandmother, Quinnie Pearl, was living in Pioche or possibly nearby Ely, which was 100 miles north of Pioche. Based on contact with Harold's mother, one or both of our young miners became interested in checking out the mining opportunities in Pioche, which was booming with postwar activity.

Welcome to Nevada

The State of Nevada is made up of more than 120 long, broad mountain ranges exhibiting rocky backbones, lifting to high altitudes, all of which run parallel from a northeast to southwest direction. If you are driving across the state from east to west or visa-versa, you traverse up and down one daunting range after another; winding all the way to the 5,000 ft. level and higher, witnessing a breath-taking view of more sky and wide open spaces than you have ever seen before; zig-zagging back down the mountain; driving straight across another barren , hot desert – which in prehistoric times was a great lake where dinosaurs roamed – just to start over again climbing the next over-sized mountain range.
 This drive becomes a spiritual odyssey to native Nevadans, and most relish the chance to do it once again, feeling an endorphin surge at the end of each trip – much like completing a marathon.
 These mountains are highly mineralized, and even as large as they are, almost every square inch has been prospected over the course of the state's 150 year history. What is more, amazingly enough, the old prospectors found most of the major ore bodies without the benefit of modern equipment – thus giving birth to a multitude of mines on the top or side of each and every one of these 120 mountain ranges.
 In the fall of 1863, a year before Nevada became a state, several Paiute Indians loaded a number of silver bearing rocks, which the Native Americans called "panacre," into a deerskin sack and took them to William Hamblin, a known local scout, prospector, and Mormon missionary. Hamblin

had been sent by the LDS church leaders to southwestern Utah to live among the Native Americans.

After some bargaining, the Indians led Hamblin to the source of the ore-bearing rock, a spot now known as Pioche, Nevada, where he discovered a wide vein of silver chloride accompanied by lead carbonate protruding to the surface of the earth. He filed the first mining claim in the area, which was formally organized in 1864, as the Meadow Valley Mining District. Prospectors started arriving post haste – actually, a sizable stampede ensued.

Mines are created by the discovery of one or more suspicious looking rocks and by following their trail straight down into the ground, resulting in a "glory hole," or straight back into the side of a mountain forming a tunnel. If more like-kind minerals are found, the glory hole will become a mine, and the miner will file a claim "forthwith" to protect his territory from other miners.

If no more minerals are found, the miner walks away with his pick and shovel, never looking back – leaving the hole open, embers still burning in the fire pit, and empty tin cans and bottles laying right where he had his last meal. There is no harder job than being a miner. It's back-breaking, physical labor in severe climates; it's terribly dangerous; and, as a business model, there is no rival with any higher risk factor. Therefore, there is no time or reason for a clean-up when your last glory hole comes up empty— grab your hat, flask, gun, and move on, buddy—"Welcome to Nevada!"

Miners Rush to Pioche

In 1868, the financier Francois Louis Alfred Pioche, a native of France, then living in San Francisco, hired Charles Hoffman to purchase property in the Meadow Valley mining District. Hoffman transported forty Mexican nationals to the area to develop mining claims and build a smelter to process the ore – separating the silver and lead from the amalgamation extracted from the ground.

The bricks for the smelter were imported from Glasgow, Scotland, and brought by ship around Cape Horn at a cost of $1.00 per brick to San Francisco. From there, they were transported by the Central Pacific Railroad probably as far as Battle Mountain, Nevada, where they were loaded into carts pulled by a mule train for several hundred miles to Pioche. As you can see, this would be an incredibly risky venture – physically and financially – and seems insane. But there was a mining fever fueled by the recent gold rush in California, and these mining men would not tolerate any "small" thinking.

In fact, Francois Lewis Alfred Pioche had the money to back up this venture. He was educated as a lawyer in France, had inherited 100,000 francs from a rich uncle, most of which had been spent pursuing an extravagant life-style in San Francisco and investing in high risk stocks. However, in the true spirit of the great American West, F.L.A. Pioche who had experienced the California gold rush, returned to France with grand stories of the wealth being made in mining on the Comstock. He attracted investors and was able to raise $6,000,000 to invest in other mining claims in the states. He purchased vast acreages in San Francisco and the Sacramento

Valley and then ventured into other mining opportunities, of which the new bonanza in the Meadow Valley District in eastern Nevada was primary.

A town was now developing around these new mines and was named after this flamboyant financier. Even in those days, it was impossible for one miner to get very far with a mining claim of any size, unless he had money to invest in labor and the equipment needed to extract the ore and transport it to a smelter for processing. Mining was, from the very beginning, a taxing enterprise requiring adequate capital, labor, and business sense.

The correct pronunciation of Pioche should be "Peoshe," with a long "e" and a soft "ch" sound, as in "champagne" and "chardonnay." But, the rough and tumble tramp-miners of the West were not familiar with the French language, had not tasted fine French wines, and were really not in the frame of mind to educate themselves in these subjects. Therefore, the name of the new mining camp became "Pioche," pronounced "Peoche," with a long "e" and a hard "ch" as in "coach" or "match,"— this pronunciation stuck.

To fully understand the random birth of this strange little town, one must realize the remoteness of its location. Pioche is 429 miles southeast from Reno and 342 miles southwest from Salt Lake City. There were no sizable towns south of Pioche, as southern Nevada was uninhabitable in the late 1800's except for the Native American tribe – the Paiutes. Only the promise of riches from precious metals could bring any civilization to this remote land where only rabbits, coyotes, mule deer and a few large mountain lions roamed.

However, news of gold and silver travels fast, even with no cell phones, computers, or telegraph lines. Mary Louise Wilcox Christian, life-long resident of Lincoln County writes,

"Denizens and nomads of the hills quickly swarmed upon the promising area. In their wake came the opportunists, tinhorn-gamblers,

gunmen, claim-jumpers, saloon-keepers, and the ladies of ill-repute. With time they were joined by a hardier breed – merchants, blacksmiths, carpenters, teamsters, teachers and ministers of the gospel. They too wanted jobs and a chance to begin anew."

All new boom-towns are prone to violence, but Pioche, due to its remote location, was even more vulnerable to lawlessness. Brute force and shoot-outs were the rule of law, evidenced by marked and unmarked graves in the local cemetery, "Boot Hill," where one full section boasts signage *"murderer's row."*

However, by 1872, the population had reached in excess of six thousand, and a heavily-bonded Courthouse with adjacent jail was under construction. The larger mines still hired gun-slingers to protect their mining claims from claim jumpers. This protection did not, however, extend to miners during their off hours, so gun-toting was still a prevailing practice.

Records show that between 1870 and 1875 there were 40 murders in Pioche with only two convictions. A predominate number of gunfighters were Irish. This was during an era of prejudice against the Irish. They couldn't get jobs, many had been orphaned during the potato famine, and they were forced to adjust to the laws of the street. Un-policed mining towns were an understandable draw for the "roughs," as they were called. Morgan Courtney, the perpetrator of multiple murders, eventually landed a job as a superintendent of a mine. The line between the law and the lawless in Pioche was, indeed, a thin one!

By 1872, the net proceeds of these mines reached $20,000,000, coming in second to the great bonanza of the Comstock mine in Virginia City. Unfortunately, F.L.A. Pioche, at the height of his mining and real estate success, committed suicide. There was no suicide note, and a presumable cause was never determined.

The early arrivers to a mining camp—the prospectors; the financiers—never bring a city planner or a zoning officer with them. No one ever actually plans to spend the rest of their life in a remote mining camp. The plan, always, is to first, figure out how to get to one of these God-forsaken places, then erect a tent, a shanty or arrange to board at a hastily-erected, drafty boarding house. Then next, file a mining claim, and dig like 'hell' until you, one day, swing that pick into a big silver deposit. Third on your list would be to pick and shovel like 'hell' for several more years to gather a nest egg. Lastly, load a couple of saddle bags full of coin onto a mule, a buckboard, a stage-coach, or if you are truly blessed, onto a train, and get the "hell" back to civilization!

Therefore, there are never any job postings for city planners in mining towns. The towns are usually situated at the top of the alluvial plains which form at the lower bases of these majestic, mineralized mountains. The miners need to be able to walk from their cabins/shanties/tents to the mine, so former footpaths blazed by the earliest miners become cart paths, which become streets. The adjacent buildings are thrown together like a wild game of "pick-up sticks," never intending to last more than a few years, as most mines are played out by that time.

Unfortunately, until the use of recent, advanced technology, when a body of ore was discovered, it was impossible to tell its dimensions – was it really large, or not? Did it extend to the east, west, south or north? Did it become smaller or larger as it extended in one of those directions? The miners could only dig in all directions until they came to the end of every side of the vein. It was a back-breaking game of inches with endless sessions of calculated guessing.

If the deposits are large enough to support mining for many years, then miners marry, have families, and the hopes and dreams for the next generation provide the impetus for folks to begin haphazardly renovating the wobbly infrastructure of the town. Big bodies or multiple big bodies of ore ultimately result in cities like Denver, Colorado and Bozeman, Montana – exceptions to the rule. Most generally, mining towns boom, grow faster than the infrastructure and then, as the ore is depleted, begin to shrink into pre-mature old age. In many cases, they die a real death, becoming a ghost town noted only in travel brochures.

In between "bonanza and borrasca," families strive to survive, and many flourish in this "survival of the fittest" environment. Children are raised profiting from a combination of lots of freedom to explore and roam, and of the discipline of parents who have had to work much harder than most to survive. To an outsider, the ramshackle looks of these mining towns belie the bonds of the community residing therein. The "ties that bind" in these communities are deep and strong, as are those in other communities where its citizens have survived great adversities and tragedies.

The mining production in Pioche ebbed and flowed, experiencing a second boom in 1909, when a spur to Pioche was added to the Los Angeles to Salt Lake City railroad line, considerably reducing the cost to ship newly-mined ore to smelters in Utah. Lower costs result in rising profits. Pioche was not dead yet!

During World War II, profitable lead-zinc deposits were developed – minerals needed for military equipment and munitions. Pioche, once again, was buzzin' with all manner of activities. Lillian Kelley, long-time resident of Pioche, noted in a Christmas article in the local newspaper,

> *"In the fall of 1942, approximately 300 soldiers, including my husband, came to work in the mines. This was necessary because most of the men who worked in the mines had been drafted, enlisted, or gone to the Pacific Coast to work in the shipyards. The government needed the lead, zinc and silver that the local mines produced... Very few houses were available, but when I arrived in November of that year with my infant daughter, my husband had found us a one-room shed."*

Fortunately, Jewel Kelley, Lillian's husband, was one of the miners who rode out the World War II boom and stuck it out during the subsequent recession, mining for years and providing well for his wife and four children, one of whom is my lifelong friend, Bobbi Jo, quoted in the introduction to this story.

The Stars Align for Jack and Virginia

During the war years and into the early 1950's, the town and its inhabitants prospered. Miners were highly paid—$13 per day. They worked hard, played hard, and spent money freely. There were a multitude of restaurants, boarding houses, hotels and a true plethora of bars – at least 17 – serving a population of approximately 1,700. There were dances every Saturday night and the bars never closed – this type of party-atmosphere only prevails when jobs are plentiful and folks have an optimistic feeling of well being.

Lee Hone, Pioche resident, recalls that as a very young man, he was making $11 per day at the "Combined Metals" mine, tending the miners' carbide lamps. He also reminisced with much chuckling about his life growing up at the Bristol mine, about 30 miles from Pioche, where his dad was mining. The family would motor to Pioche every Saturday afternoon, shop for groceries, eat at a local café, go to the movies, and then the adults would hit the bars for drinking and dancing. The kids would play up and down Main Street with all the other miner's children until 10:00 p.m., when the cops would patrol up and down the street barking, "*All you kids get in your cars now. It's 10:00.*"

The parents always stocked the cars with pillows and blankets for this occasion, and the kids would curl up in the back seat and go to sleep while their parents and all of the other parents danced the night away in the infamous "Alamo Club." Imagine— the local police acted as "night nurse" for all the partying miner's kids!

Actually, times haven't changed that much. I attended a Homecoming football game in 2014, in Panaca, Nevada, where I observed at least 50 small children running up and down the sidelines over and under the bleachers for several hours without intervention from one adult. I never did figure out who even one of those kids belonged to. I love Lincoln County!

It was during this free-wheeling period of time that Jack Brown rode into town. The family says that Jack met Virginia Pistone, his future bride, at a Saturday night dance during the summer of 1947. We don't know if it was a Saturday night in June, July or August, but we do know that it was the fourth of July for Jack and Virginia. Fire crackers exploded, the stars aligned in perfect formation, and a great love ensued between the young soldier and this diminutive, feisty, dark-eyed, 19- year-old Italian girl.

Life at the Pioche Hotel

Virginia Katherine Pistone was born March 9, 1928, in San Francisco, Ca. to Virginia Eugenia Tira Cottino Pistone and Pietro Pistone, both Italian nationals. The senior Virginia was born in 1881, in Italy, and she had a sister who had immigrated to the United States, as had Virginia's boyfriend. Her parents agreed to send her to live with her sister, expecting that she would marry the boyfriend, Guido Cottino. They purchased a first class ticket for Virginia Eugenia on a ship to America and said their goodbyes as Virginia sailed away to the "land of the free." Unfortunately, the ship's management took advantage of this young Italian girl traveling alone and put her in the "hold" for the entire trip, using her 1st class birth for another guest!

The young Virginia Eugenia Tira survived the horrible sea journey and made her way to Montana to join her sister. She did, indeed, marry her childhood boyfriend, Guido Cottino, now a Butte, Montana miner. Virginia Eugenia gave birth to four children during their years in Butte. Unfortunately, a terrible influenza swept through the town in 1908, and all four of their children died within a two week period, leaving the couple childless.

The Cottino's heard about the booming mines in Delamar, Nevada, fifty-four miles south of Pioche. Perhaps, the grieving process spurred the desire for a new mine in a warmer climate. The couple moved to Delamar, where Guido worked in the mine, and Virginia, a superb cook, opened an Italian bakery. In her spare time, she also managed to give birth to Irma, Victor, Lillian, Albert and Domenico. The Cottino household was once again filled with the tiny voices and running footsteps of children.

When the mine in Delamar played out, the town declined rapidly, quickly becoming a true ghost town. The couple moved to Pioche where Guido became employed at the Combined Metals Reduction Company Number 1 mine. They also rented a large boarding house on the south or upside of "Main" street, which Virginia managed, along with keeping tabs on the five little Cottino's. The boarding house had been built during the original Pioche boom in the late 1860's.

On April 8, 1924, Guido and Virginia purchased the "Pioche Hotel" from E.W. and Ada Holdaway. Later, during the 1920's, Guido passed away, and Virginia was alone with the full responsibility of the hotel and five children.

A family friend, Pietro Pistone, also an Italian national and bachelor, worked at the Number 1 mine with Guido. He lived in a miner's cabin close to the hotel and had been a close friend of the family and a regular fixture at the hotel.

Virginia and Pietro decided to join forces and to marry. Pietro had family in South San Francisco, so the newlyweds, seeking a better way of life, packed up this large family and moved. While living in San Francisco, Virginia gave birth to her last child (Pietro's only child) – a petite baby girl who became her namesake, "Virginia Katherine."

The couple decided to return to Pioche after several years in the Bay area and, once again, moved back into the hotel with their now even larger family. All of the grandchildren remember huge family gatherings at the hotel every Christmas where they would run up and down the stairs and through all the halls chasing one another, totally ignoring the pleas of their parents to "settle down." A grandson, Tom Brown, remembers fondly his grandmother's rolls and Uncle D's rigatoni, *"The smell alone was worth the price of a room!"*

The hotel, on the main street of Pioche, was in close proximity to the Number 1 mine and all the cafes and bars. This was the home address of Virginia's baby girl, Virginia Katherine. From her toddler years until her marriage to Jack Brown, young Virginia Jr. resided at the Pioche Hotel, Main Street, Pioche, Nevada, with her parents, five half-siblings, all manner of hotel guests, and a variety of "pay-by-the-week" miners.

Virginia Sr. was no fool, and she knew the success of the hotel depended on its reputation. She would not allow these miners to act out in any way in her establishment. Local residents, Muff and Vern Stever, recall that when they came to Pioche as newlyweds, they were asked for their marriage license before Mrs. Cottino-Pistone would rent them a room!

Young Virginia enjoyed a great life growing up in this active atmosphere. Being vivacious and gregarious by nature, she enjoyed having lots of people around her – the perfect child to be raised in a hotel. She loved to dance and would perform her own choreography on the sidewalk in front of the hotel, much to the enjoyment of the resident miners, who would gratefully throw nickels to encourage the talented youngster.

In her teen years, Virginia became proficient with a baton and won the coveted "drum majorette" position with the Lincoln County High School marching band, performing in far-away places such as the Heldorado Parade in Las Vegas! Some readers might worry about the welfare of such an adorable young girl being raised in this wild mining town in a hotel inhabited by itinerant miners. But we must remember that Virginia was also living with the "Italian Army," made up of brothers, Vic, Albert and Domenico (Dee), as well as two sisters who adored her. Any man making an untoward advance to their baby sister would not see the light of the next dawn, and no questions would be asked in Pioche – there are lots of glory holes in those surrounding hills!

Jack Brown was 26 when he and Virginia met. She was 19 – a fair age difference. However, being raised in a large family and exposed to so many different people, Virginia was self-assured beyond her years. She could hold her own with the handsome newcomer. Jack was interested in marriage fairly early in the relationship. He had been through the war, had traveled, and was ready to settle into a permanent relationship, but Virginia had made a self-imposed rule that she would not marry until she turned 21. She held firm to this decision, turned twenty-one in March of 1949, and married Jack Brown one month later on April 2, at nearby Ely, Nevada.

Jack Brown was short of stature – maybe 5'5" or 5'6", with Hollywood good looks. He was extroverted, as reported by several family friends, and a "great dancer." Virginia, who stood at barely 5 ft. in her stocking feet, thought Jack was tall and, boy, did she love to dance. They were a stunning couple on the dance floor—dancing every Saturday night, preferably to the wee hours of Sunday morning. They both loved the outdoors and would take any opportunity to go camping and fishing. Jack loved to fly-fish.

Jack and Virginia were young, in love, and living in a mining boom town with many other young, optimistic couples – my parents being one of those couples. I remember my parents hosting many parties in our small house during the winter months. The women would make their own cocktail dresses from Vogue patterns purchased in nearby Cedar City, Utah. There were lots of steak fry events in the nearby hills when the weather was good; parties at the Fire Hall; meetings and social gatherings for the Masons, the Eastern Star, Oddfellows, and Rebecca's— and always dancing at the Alamo Club every Saturday night. There was never a lack of social activities in a working mining town – miners work hard, play hard, and set a high standard for those around them.

Jack was making good money at Combined Metals Reduction Company, known for fair wages and treating their miners with respect. It was a great time to be living in the United States of America. We had just won a great war; the economy was booming; and, Jack and Virginia were living the American dream.

On Oct 30, 1949, Virginia gave birth to Dorothy (Dottie) Katherine, named after Jack's only sister. On Oct. 11, 1950, Thomas Eugene was born, to be followed in very short order by baby sister, Dawna Kristine, born Aug. 28, 1951. Jack and Virginia had three children within 21 months, and they were both thrilled.

Since Virginia's mother had a total of ten children, rapid childbirth did not seem unusual to our young bride. And, by accounts of several nieces, nephews and neighbors, Jack loved children. Nephew, Guy Cottino remembers, *"He used to pin me down and tickle me until I was crazy with laughter."* Niece, Annette Urquhart recalled visiting the Browns in Pioche and going on a family hike. She writes,

"Annette had a fairly new pair of moccasins on and for whatever reason removed her shoes and continued hiking barefoot. The shoes were left behind and—out of sight, out of mind—lost. Jack, patiently and supportively led a search in an effort to find the shoes. All these years later, Annette cannot remember whether the shoes were found —- a much more impressive memory is the strong feelings of a child who was loved and taken seriously by her uncle Jack."

Becky Goodman, Harold Goodman's step-daughter, offered what information she could to help pin down the timeline and whereabouts of Jack and Harold during the several years following the war. Harold had told Becky and her brother, Lee, that he had worked at Combined Metals Number 1 mine with Jack, but that he had told Jack he was quitting because he thought the mine was just too dangerous.

Harold met May Jean in Sept. of 1947, in Park City, Utah, and they were married within 6 weeks – Oct. 18, 1947. This was six months after Jack Brown hired on at Combined Metals (April 28, 1947.) The most likely scenario seems to be that Jack and Harold traveled to Pioche to seek employment at Combined Metals based on information from Harold's mother, Quinnie Pearl. Harold probably made the decision within several months that this was not the mine for him, left Pioche, and went to mine in Park City, Utah, as he was married by October. Further support of this timeline is that I was never able to find anyone in Pioche who knew Harold, which lead me to believe that his stay there had to be a short stop.

May Jean, at the time of her marriage to Harold, had a nine-month-old daughter, Becky, from a prior marriage. They purchased a house in Park City, Utah and had a child of their own, Lee. Harold adopted Becky when she was seven, and he was the only father she ever knew – or wanted to know, according to Becky. Harold and his family ultimately moved back to Arizona due to the health of their son, Lee. Harold worked the rest of his career underground in the Miami and Superior, Arizona copper mines, which were safer mines than those in Pioche, due the nature of the sedimentation surrounding the "pay dirt."

Combined Metals No.1 Mine

The Pioche "Mother Lode" of ore, first identified by the Paiute Indians in 1863, which produced $20,000,000 worth of silver, was a strike of approximately 3,000 ft. wide and was 1,200 ft. below the surface. The raw ore contained such a high content of gold, silver and lead, that it could be transported by wagons pulled by teams of horses or mules for hundreds of miles across the rocky desert and still produce a handsome profit for the mine-owners and stockholders.

This body of ore was embedded in a "friable quartz gangue" (quartzite) and could be easily extracted. But when the mother vein was exhausted in a decade, Pioche fell on hard times, almost succumbing to the fate of Delamar, Hamilton, Fay, Tybo, and many other ghost towns. The difference was that Pioche had become the county seat of Lincoln County, and a large ranching and livestock industry had developed north of Pioche along the Utah boarder, keeping the small town afloat.

In 1912, more experiments with the non-precious metals of lead and zinc were undertaken. Ed Snyder, a graduate of the Michigan School of Mines, developed an interest in the mines around Pioche, leased several properties and began experimenting with the combined lead/zinc ores. The problem was how to extract, refine, and transport the quantities that existed below the 1,200 ft. level, where excessive amounts of water must be extracted.

In 1923, Snyder acquired a reliable backer, National Lead Company. They provided the quality geologists who methodically probed this mountain until 1930, when they came up with the best answer—sinking a shaft on the opposite side of the mountain (the Caselton side of the Ely range) where the more gradual slopes provided better access to the ore bodies and an easier way to drain water.

In late 1940, with a reliable supply of electricity from Hoover Dam, the company built a flotation mill near-by with a 800 ton crushing plant and a 400 ton flotation unit. This was all that was needed to wake up the sleepy town, and Pioche was booming once again!

After consulting several mining geology studies of Treasure Hill, I concluded that the miner, Hyrum Hansen, has in layman's terms given the best description of the geology of this mountain,

"The ore bed of the Castleton and Number 1 mines were characterized by a 'lower bed' over which was a hard limestone 'rib' layer. Above the rib was the 'upper bed' and above that was what they called 'black lime' which was not solid rock but was a rather soft, kind of greasy, crumbly stuff of no commercial value. Further up was solid limestone and other layering. The lower bed was close to a five-foot thickness. The rib was two to three feet thick (no commercial value, of course) and the upper bed varied greatly in depth but was generally thicker than the lower bed. The mine's objective was to remove the lower bed, the rib and the upper bed. The size of this treasure trove of lead-zinc ore was a few miles long by perhaps a mile wide.

"When freshly blasted, the lower ore bed would be described best as a beautiful metallic crystalline structure that brightly glistened when a light was played on it......Over time this galena material would oxidize and become rather dull and dark gray....The upper ore bed was a finer grain crystalline material that looked like a rich metal but which just wasn't as dazzling to the eye.

"As it happens, it was not possible to just go in and take all of that material out without doing something to prevent the rock above from crashing down. So they periodically left large 'pillars' for temporary support. The plan included pulling out these pillars as they backed out once the main body of ore had been exhausted. Some might think the extensive timbering was what was to hold it all up, but such a feeble

structure would not do the job. The timber served to provide protection from small falling rocks and to aid in getting in position to drill and do the other things that were part of a mining activity....

"Eventually, as the mountains were gradually thrust up and great and extensive faulting occurred, the once level bed had vertical fault separations between sections so that parts were at 300 ft., at 600 ft., at 840 ft., at 960 ft., at 1,200 ft., and at 1,400 ft., as measured from the collar of the Caselton shaft.

"A drift on the 1,200 ft. level connected the Caselton and #1 shafts. This drift (tunnel to the layman) was completed sometime in the 40's and was regarded as something of a great fete because of the accuracy with which the two parts of the drift met about midway between the two shafts, which were about six miles apart. Their meeting point was about six inches off from each other."

I was able to determine from a government geology study published in 1932 that the "black lime," named by the miners was officially "black sphalerite." Due to the greasy feel of these crumbly rocks, the miners also called it "black slime." This layer of sediment was truly insidious. It was not worth anything, and it was always in the way, causing trouble for the miners due to its instability – a miner's worst nightmare.

In the early days of mining the Number 1, the air was bad, the ore was crumbly, the hours were long, and it was dreadfully dark. Darrel Free, a miner of the 1930's and husband of Irma Cottino, Virginia's half sister, recalls in his oral history,

"Bad ground, bad air – it was terrible. We'd be working there and it was caving around us all the time. We had carbide lights of course. It would blow the lights out and the concussion would roll us down the drift....The headaches were terrible. It would take a lot out of you."

Question: *What did you do for your headaches? Did you use ammonia?*

Darrel: "*Yes, we all carried the capsules.*"

Question: "*Was it caving in because it was old and the timbers were old, or what?*"

Darrel: "*It's just natural. You open enough area and there are seams and cracks and fissures.*"

Question: *Why didn't they leave more pillars?*

Darrel: "*They wanted more tons.*"

Question: "*Combined Metals were basically exploiting men, weren't they?*"

Darrel: "*They pushed their men some. That's the way they had to do it in those days. The ore in there wasn't high grade.*"

This passage says it all – an entrepreneur with a huge investment trying to operate a business in the black against large odds, and men needing and willing to take risks with their lives to provide something extra for their families.

Luckily by the time Jack Brown signed on with Combined Metals in 1947, unions had been established, and the working conditions were somewhat better. The mines were electrified, the tools were mechanized to some degree, the ventilation was improved, and the miners were paid a living wage with time and a half for the 6th day worked each week. (A typical miner's work week was 48 hours, and this was standard in every mine in the West.)

No One Could Out-Produce Jack Brown

By 1953, Jack Brown had been working in the Number 1 and Caselton mines for six full years – six days a week. He knew that mine like the back of his hand, and he knew his job and how to go about it efficiently. His short stature and agility worked in his favor in the mine – using large machinery in tight spaces. What's more, Jack, unlike many miners, had no fear or trepidation while underground. He owned this country and moved through the tunnels, rises and shafts like a panther. Jack was totally in charge of his environment. This was not true of every miner. Miner, Merrill Barnum, recalls in his oral interview:

"One morning I got up there and the fellow who usually got there first (I worked where he was working) was back out of the way. I said, 'What's the matter? You don't feel good today?' He says, 'No, I've kind of lost my nerve. And if you sit down here and listen a little while, you'll lose yours, too.'"

Jack had undoubtedly started as a "mucker" and worked his way up to a "miner." No one gets hired anytime, at any mine, as a miner without proving himself as a mucker for quite some time. A mucker is one who shovels and loads the ore on carts for removal from the mine after the miners have blasted. Miners always work in pairs as partners. In the mining world they are always referred to in the "Old West" vernacular of "pardners."

The pardners are shown where to work by the mining shift boss or foreman, but then it is up to their discretion to efficiently separate the ore from its matrix so it can be extracted. They discuss the goal at hand, tap with hammers all around the identified ore and listen. The sounds caused by the tapping tell the miners whether the matrix is solid. This sounds very unscientific to the novice, but the fact is that this method had been used quite effectively for hundreds of years by miners all over the world. A good miner is a good listener, for sure, and there has to be full confidence between two pardners, as both lives depend on their joint decisions as to where to blast and how much powder to use. This is really serious business, and no one in the mine wants an unqualified miner working on his shift. For these reasons, there is absolutely no drinking of alcohol in a mine, and it is quite frowned upon for a miner to even come to work with a hangover.

John Franks, Pioche resident and mine "hoistman," recounts in his oral history:

"Being a good miner is a real profession....It was just a matter of breaking the ground with the least amount of holes —placing the holes so they broke clean...Well a burn is where you drill a group of holes together and blow that out first...but a lot of this ground breaks real well. You put in what you call your cuts and shoot those first...you have your cuts, your breast holes, your back holes, and then your relievers maybe and then your lifters...Boy, I worked around one or two and they made every move count. I admired them... they would think ahead to what they were going to need and have it available when they needed it."

This was Jack Brown in a nutshell. Because of his constellation of aptitudes, Jack quickly realized that he could make more money working "gyppo" than hourly. "Gyppo" is a mining term for "piece work." The word is a derivative of the word "gypsy", alluding to the independence of the miner.

In other words, Jack Brown was one fast dude at producing the most usable ore per shift, and he was reaping financial rewards for his abilities by working "gyppo." Jack

Brown had a plan. He knew the ore would diminish in time – it always does – metals are not renewable; that this mine was not as safe as some, due to the consistency of the aggregates; and that he needed to eventually adopt a new career. Jack Brown was planning on eventually moving his family back to Arizona and buying a small ranch. He had been raised in a ranching area and knew he could make a go of it. Once he had a wife, three babies, and an exit plan, Jack Brown became a driven miner. No one could out-produce Jack Brown.

Around 1950, the demand for lead and zinc started to decline, which resulted in falling prices for both. More tonnage was needed to produce the same profit. Jack was forced to accept the hourly wages and could not make the extra money working "gyppo" as he had before.

The mining production and gross profits for Combined Metals Reduction Company from the late 1940's to 1954 were as follows:

1947	18,750 tons	$5,388,400 gross revenue
1950	27,389 tons	$8,493,900 " "
1953	9,168 tons	$2,723,900 " "
1954	2,258 tons	$766,700 " "

These numbers show the not so gradual decline of the Combined Metals Number 1 Mine. The future was clear to management and also to the miners. They understood the future of this mine.

On March 14, 1953, Virginia made dinner for the family as usual and packed a lunch bucket for Jack, as she had been doing six days a week for the past four years. Jack was due to clock in at the Caselton mine at 6:00 p.m., which was about a fifteen minute drive from their house. The miners always left for their shift in street clothes with their lunch box. When they reached the mine, they would change in to their work dungarees (diggers), leaving the street clothes in a locker. At the end of the shift, they would take a shower at the mine and change back into their street clothes to return home. Miners never left the mine covered in dust. (Only in the movies!)

Jack would then have "clocked in" and moved his brass medallion to the "in-board" before entering the lift to be hoisted down to the 940 level. Based on other oral interviews with miners, I believe that once Jack arrived at the 940 level, he would have walked 10 to 20 minutes in the tunnel to reach the area where they were working that shift.

Bobbi Jo Kelley Ebel, daughter of miner Jewell Kelley, recalled, "*Daddy never came home dirty from the mine. He always came home showered, in clean clothes and smelling good.*" These miners always entered their homes after their shift looking like they had been selling insurance all day. The dirt of the mine stayed at the mine, and families were spared any reminders that daddy works in a hot, dirty, sometimes unsafe environment. The underground world of the miners was, and is, kept among the miners – a band of brothers.

By 9:45 p.m. Jack Brown and his "pardner," Vern Ceal were working at the 940 J "rise" in "stope" 5663 of the Caselton mine, preparing to "*stand a set of timber in the stope.*" The 940 "rise" means the 940 ft. level. Jack and Vern were blasting and clearing an opening in the rock to install a set of timber. One set would be 5 ft. 4 inches. The "back" of the tunnel, which means the height or ceiling, was about 7 ft. The first round of explosive did not open enough ground for the size of the timber. The pardners discussed the situation and elected to drill three more holes in order to set off a second round of explosives needed to gain additional room for the posts. After the second blast, a large slab of solid rock about 7ft .X 5ft. X 3 to 4 ft. thick, (probably about 1,000 lbs.) sloughed off the hanging wall of the tunnel coming down directly onto Jack Brown, which killed him instantly. Jack was 31 years old.

Johnny Reese, the shift boss, reported,

Q. "*What means did you use to recover the body?*"

A. *"We tried to haul it off with the slusher, and all we did was break the cable, so we broke it in small pieces and got it off."*

Further questions with Johnny Reese are as follows:

Q. *"Had you made an examination of the ground?"*
A. *"Yes, I did when I first went in that morning."*
Q. *"And was there any faulting in that section of the mine?"*
A. *"Yes, it was commencing to get into the fault."*
Q. *"In this particular stope did you make any comments in regard to the ground, or any instructions as to the drilling?'*
A. *"No Sir, not that night. Jack and I have both been in that country a lot, and we knew it was bad ground, and Jack realized it."*
Q. *"Was it unduly bad in there?"*
A. *"No worse than it had been, but it is ground that you have to keep timbered up."*
Q. *"What is your regard for Jack as a miner."*
A. *"A number 1."*
Q. *"He had the habit of being very careful?"*
A. *"Yes sir."*
Q. *"Had he had occasion to work in that particular type of ground for any length of time?"*
A. *"He blocked that country out, and then it was shut down for a period and then he went back over there."*

Further questions with Jack's pardner, Vern Ceal, are as follows. I believe that Jack and Vern had been pardners for quite some time.

Q. *"So you had to have another 30 or 40 inches to make room for another set?"*
A. *"Yes."*
Q. *"And you shot three plugs?"*
A. *"Yes sir."*
Q. *"Was there anything unusual in the ground?"*
A. *"We both debated on it,— we knew it was dangerous."*

Q. "Did you hear Jack make any comments with regard to the condition of the ground?"
A. "Not anymore than always. He just said let's get our muck out and timber."
Q. "Did he examine it?"
A. "Oh, yes."
A. "Yes, as far as we could see there was nothing in there."
Q. "Did you make any suggestions to Jack?"
A. "I told him there was a jump-up in the ore and we better look it over."

From an interview with fellow miner, Bill Eddards:

"I was working within about 15 or 18 ft. of where Jack was working, and I heard a big rock fall, and I turned around and looked and hollered to see if he was all right, but there was no answer. My pardner and I went in there, and all we could see was the battery off his light, and I knew he was under it, and we proceeded to get help to get him out."

Q. "Did it fall in one piece?"
A. "One piece."
Q. "And was it the iron capping?"
A. "Mostly black slime."
Q. "Would you think the ground was worse than usual?"
A. "I don't think so,—Jack was a good miner."

Black Slime – the Wild Card

An inquest was held on Monday, March 16, 1953, by the Justice of the Peace, Rex Bentley. It appears that Mr. Bentley was also the acting coroner. The following people were questioned about the accident.

Bill Eddards: a fellow miner working 15 to 18 ft. from Jack at the time of the accident.
Johnny Reese: the shift boss on duty
Vernon Ceal: Jack's pardner
Dewey Sullivan: The mine safety inspector.

The cause of the accident on the *"Employer's Report of Accident to Employee"* filed with the State Inspector of Mines was, *"Cleaning out hitch for post when a large slab of rock fell out of back – causing fatal injuries."* The accident was noted as *"Unavoidable."*

In other words, it appears to me that this accident was indeed, "unavoidable," as long as we accept the premise that minerals must be extracted from large mountains even if they are embedded in loose crumbly black rock like *"black slime."* This premise should be given some sincere soul-searching by all of us. What price should be paid for the advancement of industry? Who should pay the price?

Virginia's father had worked all of his life in various mines and had, in fact, been a shift boss in the Number 1 mine during the 20's. Two of her three brothers had worked at the Number 1 and/or Caselton mine. But that night when her three brothers drove up in front of her house, Virginia thought surely that something was wrong with her mother. Understandably, Virginia Brown was shocked and totally inconsolable. She was twenty-four years old and now alone with three children, ages three-and-a-half, two-and-a-half, and one.

A funeral was held at the LDS Chapel in Pioche on Wednesday, March 18th, and interment was at the Catholic Cemetery with graveside services held by The American Legion. Virginia remained inconsolable for several months. Her brother and sister-in-law, Vic and Agnes Cottino, took the three Brown children into their home for about a month to give Virginia time alone to grieve – she was so young.

Later, after the children returned to their mother, the family discovered that Virginia was leaving the house late at night after the kids went to sleep, driving to the cemetery, and lying on top of Jack's grave for hours. This large family handled the problem beautifully by taking turns going to her house in the middle of the night and watching the babies until Virginia returned from her nocturnal wandering.

In later years, Virginia told her children that several months after Jack's death, while sleeping during the wee hours of the morning, Jack appeared at the side of her bed and told her not to worry about him, as he was o.k. and was, in fact, happy. He instructed her that she needed to pull herself together – that she had a job to do – that she had to raise these three children, and he knew that she could do it.

Our young Virginia resolved that day to, indeed, pull herself together and to be the very best mother that she could be – and she did and she was! She filed for Social Security for dependents, which was $100 per month per child at that time. The miners took up a collection for the family, which also helped considerably. Whether her brothers and sisters helped her financially, no one knows. They are all deceased and none ever spoke of this to their children, nor did Virginia ever speak about money to her children. Combined Metals paid the wages they owed to Jack Brown for time worked until his death, but they did not contribute anything to the family. Mining companies did not provide death or disability payments to employees during this period. They paid higher wages than most other industries to compensate for the risks, but that is all that they offered.

Virginia never worked, priding herself on staying at home, keeping a very close watch over her children, cooking great meals, and maintaining a spotless house. Jack's post-death visit had set the stage for Virginia's future, and she held a steady course.

Virginia did re-marry about three years later to Lewis Gordon. She dealt with her continued grief by attending to other people in the community who were going through any emotional upheaval. She practically owned stock in "Hallmark," says her daughters, as she was sending cards continually. She profoundly felt the pain of others and realized wisely that by ministering to them, she was strengthened.

All three Brown children have led successful and rewarding lives. Dottie and Dawna both married and raised successful children. Tom graduated from college with a criminal justice degree, but after a gun fight with some bad guys in the first year of his employment with Metro police in Las Vegas, he pulled up stakes and returned to Lincoln County. Mining, at that point, looked much safer.

Virginia told him if he ever went underground, she would never sleep again, so Tom honored that and always worked in the mills above ground. However, while servicing a windmill in 1975, his safety belt broke, sending him downward 30 ft., breaking 3 vertebrae and one shoulder. The Division of Forestry started looking very good after that, and Tom worked for them for nineteen years until his retirement. He resides in Pioche where he enjoys all of the old mining stories and those who, so colorfully, spin the tales.

The entire town mourned Jack Brown's death. When people live in a "company town" where everyone's livelihood is affected by one industry, and where danger lurks behind every rock, the inter dependence of the individuals becomes greater. The loss of one of their own is felt deeply and does not ever go away. I can attest to this based on my own feelings and by the reactions of other residents whom I have interviewed. Bobbi Jo Kelley Ebel's father worked at the Caselton mine at the time of the accident – he had been on day shift. She remembers when the sirens first started blaring that her dad got dressed and took off for the mine. Every miner in town would have been involved in the recovery of Jack Brown's body. The next day, Bobbi asked her mother, *"What's wrong with daddy?"* She remembers her mother telling her, *"Daddy is very upset about Mr. Brown's death, and he doesn't want to talk about it."*

Every child in the town lost innocence that day; every wife was cruelly reminded that she too could be a widow at any time; every miner was faced with new awareness that he was going to work tomorrow in a big black hole in the ground where large rocks could fall at any moment, and he too could be at the wrong place at the wrong time ending up underneath a ton of quartzite.

The metals that we remove from these deep dark holes are, for the most part, very beneficial to our society in multitudes of ways. However, we must remember that there is "no free lunch," especially when it comes to the environment. Mother Nature does not give up her hidden jewels easily, and when they are taken from her, a potentially collapsible void is created, which will not be filled naturally for another 10,000 years.

Therefore, mining is an industry that must be accompanied by a very large sense of responsibility by all of its participants, especially by management and by the governments who regulate them, as it will be the miners who pay the ultimate price when things go wrong inside a mine.

Jack Brown

Harold and Jack

Dottie, Virginia, Dawna (Baby), Tommy, Jack

Virginia

WIDOW'S LAMENT

By
Richard Brautigan

*"It's not quite cold enough
To go borrow some firewood
From the neighbors."*

ROSCOE HAMILTON WILKES

Nevada Miner

Roscoe Writes Home

"When whipporwills call, evenin' is nigh,
Hurry to my Blue Heaven.
Turn to the right, there's a little white light,
Will lead you to my Blue Heaven."

Roscoe Hamilton Wilkes whistles and sings intermittently as he slaps his straight razor against the leather strop sharpening the blade to a fine edge. Roscoe had barbered some in the past between mining jobs, and he prided himself on a close shave. He was also one to keep his mustache and hair trimmed decently, even if he was living in a boarding house packed with rough miners.

Such was the case on this 27th day of August, 1928, when Roscoe was preparing for a hot meal in the dining room of the newly built boarding house in Tybo, Nevada – intending to write home to his wife and kids after supper. Roscoe was 51 years old and partially deaf – two major disadvantages for a hard-rock miner, but he hadn't given up yet. He had made his way to Tybo, the latest Nevada boomtown, as he had done repeatedly dozens of times during the past thirty years – and, as always, he was optimistic about his future. After all, Roscoe Hamilton Wilkes was a miner, and optimism runs deep in this profession.

The letter written on that hot August evening remained in my grandmother's box of important papers until her death and was saved by my father. It reads as follows:

Dear Wife and Kids,

I am finally located so I will drop you a line. I could not get anything in Ely that I would have so I came over here. This place is 100 miles from Ely and 70 miles from Tonopah. This is an old time town. But all of the old stuff is just about gone. This is going to be one of the neatest camps in the state. They are putting up some of the best buildings here I ever saw. This far from a Rail Road. Have just moved into the new Boarding house and it is sure nice. They are now putting the furniture in the new Bunk house and it looks like a swell Hotel. Everything to be steam Heat. Hot and Cold Water Electricity toilets and Bath. 7 other Buildings now going up – change Room, office, machine shop and Dwellings all under construction and they are excavating for a Big Mill. They have 100 men here and want 50 more. Want a lot of carpenters. I have worked 4 days and get $5.00 per day. I was offered $6.00 per day to do steeple Jack work on a Gallows frame. I may take it yet if I can get some tennis shoes. They have no store here yet as they have no Building for it – Everything has to be ordered from Tonopah 70 miles.

There are no vacant houses now But may be some when they move into the new Bunk house.

Ros

Tybo, Nev

Send any mail for me here. There is a swede here doing some hair cutting of nights But he won't shave at all. He is a ditch digger of day times. I am doing Roust about work But don't have to carry any Rail Road Rails. I helped carpenters today. I spoke to the Supt. today for a job as janitor in the new Bunk house. He was very nice, and said he thought they could find me something pretty good just a little later.

How is everything in Pioche. Tell me all the news. Hope you are all well and getting along good. No use for you to holler at me for money. I will send you the first I get. Tell me about everybody.

Love to you all,
Ros
Send any mail to me here.

Oh Grandma! (early 1960's)

One bitter-cold Friday evening in January, a few close friends gathered with my family in our small dining/family room. There was just enough room for a small love seat and a black and white T.V., as well as the table and chairs, which made it double as a family room. I'm sure the wind was blowing, because the wind always blows most of the winter in Pioche.

We were celebrating my dad's birthday and had been enjoying lively conversation over cocktails followed by pot roast, mashed potatoes and brown gravy. I was a teenager—sipping Seven-Up, of course.

The conversation waned slightly as we all sat back in our chairs to let our stomachs settle a bit before the chocolate cake was served. Our birthday cakes were usually smothered with swirls of fluffy, white, carefully boiled to a perfect soft-ball stage, frosting. It tasted like divinity candy – my favorite – and was difficult to make, failed to set up if the humidity was high.

Rita Hardy, the wife of Newmont geologist, Byran Hardy, turned to my grandmother and, trying to draw her into the conversation, graciously inquired, "*Mrs. Wilkes, tell us about your husband. What was he like?*"

Grandma basked in the glow of a cocktail and the intimate gathering, fully forgetting that she and her husband had fought like cats and dogs as they traversed the western United States and Mexico from one mine to the next for ten years, ultimately separating, which left her stranded with two kids and no means of support in the most remote Nevada mining camp of them all. She replied with great flourish,

"Oh, he was just beautiful; and, whenever he went to the 'sportin' house', all the women would just rave!"

My dad and my aunt were, understandably, speechless, while the rest of us laughed until our sides split.

Ohhhh, grandma!

Welcome to life in the mining camps of the Wild West, where prohibition was never noticed, prostitution was legal, and families laughed about it over dessert.

The Missing Grandpa

We all have four grandparents, but most of us never experience knowing all four. Whether we like them, whether we have anything in common with them is irrelevant. It's just good to know one's kin. We learn so much about what we want and don't want by observing our relatives up close and personal.

If you know or knew all four of your grandparents, consider yourself blessed. The worth and measure of the knowing are beyond my capabilities at description. I feel lucky to have known three of my four grandparents, and I knew each of them very well.

My mother's parents owned a dairy farm ten miles north of Yuba City, California, and remained on their farm until their deaths at ages 86 and 95. Clara Viney only left California two times in her entire life, which were trips to Pioche to see us. Marion Lawrence Viney traveled on a troop train from Sacramento to Newport News, Virginia, towards the end of World War I. He was on a ship to France when dysentery overtook the entire ship, and they were ordered to return to shore. Luckily, for all of the soldiers on that ship, the war ended before their recovery was complete, and they were dismissed by Uncle Sam. After that, Grandpa never wanted to venture farther than the Roseville livestock auction, and he pretty much made that rule stick.

During the 1950's, the levy broke on the Feather River near Marysville, California, and the whole county was flooded up to the rooftops. My grandparents, in their 60's, lost all of their livestock and farming equipment. The house and barn were fortunately repairable. Most people would have taken the insurance settlement and moved to town. My grandparents bought all new livestock and equipment and started over from scratch – true grit and a testament to the fact that the life they had chosen was the right one for both of them.

From these grandparents, I observed a lifestyle of steadfast determination which valued the land, its people, and all animal life over and above worldly goods. I observed that a person could live a very full life planting oneself in one spot and not moving but a few acres in either direction. However, I was not sure if this would be a fit for me. Actually, I was pretty convinced at a young age that milking cows twice a day was great fun for one week a year, but not a lifestyle I could maintain.

Then, of course, there was my paternal grandmother, quoted in the introduction to this story. Grandma, Estella Maud Neal, (aka. Betty Wilkes,) was a force to be reckoned with and a woman of many contradictions.

Her given name, Estella Maud, was a beautiful, stately name befitting any duchess. Yet, she preferred to adopt the stage name, as it were, of Betty. She was never on the stage, but she somehow envisioned herself with a more casual, modern name. Anyway, after moving ten to fifteen times from one mining camp to the next, who was to know her real name, and what did it matter? She felt very successful and youthful as a "Betty," and in time, she even shortened the Betty to "Bett," and that name stuck.

Grandma Bett was born near Bolivar, Missouri, on a family farm, as were most people in the late 1800's. She lived with her parents until she was married at age 26, which would have been considered at that time an "old maid." Her photos show a beautiful young woman, but knowing her as I did, I can imagine that she was a combination of too picky and too cantankerous to be good marriage material. However, my grandfather, Roscoe Hamilton Wilkes, who was fourteen years older than she— age 40 at the time they married—came calling and figured he could handle her. I am sure that within a short time he must have realized that he had misjudged his taming abilities, but they married in Joplin, Missouri on May 10, 1917.

Roscoe and Bett traveled the West always on the lookout for a better paying mine; but, ten years later, grandma was forced to grow roots once again when she and her husband separated, leaving her stranded in Pioche, Nevada, a very remote mining camp 173 miles due north of Las Vegas. It was 1930, and she was living in a two room miner's cabin with her two children, Roscoe Jr. and Kathryn. Grandma was destined to remain in that miner's cabin long after the children had grown and left home.

When my parents, Roscoe Harold, and his wife, Alberta (Bertie) moved back to Pioche in 1948, Grandma, still in the miner's cabin, became my daytime baby sitter while both my parents worked. She did not trust many people – actually, pretty much no one – so she would not allow me to play with any other children in her neighborhood.

However, and here comes the first contradiction, she insisted on paying her respects to any family who lost a loved one by attending the funeral – and there were no exceptions. Therefore, I accompanied grandma to every funeral and viewing subsequent to every death that occurred in Pioche. I guess we could draw the conclusion that she liked dead people better than those still living. It makes sense – the dead don't talk back.

My dad's pleas to "*stop taking Karen to funerals*" fell on deaf ears, so I had seen more dead bodies by the time I was four than most people see in a lifetime. You may wonder whether that warped my developing psyche. Well, the answer is that it did not. I have a very healthy, realistic view of death and am a firm believer in leaving a little extra money when I die for the best hair dresser and make-up artist in the area, as Grandma and I would spend plenty of time viewing the deceased women while Grandma analyzed how they looked....Oh, Grandma!

And could this Grandma swear – she could out-swear any miner in town. The upshot was that Grandma protected me from the outside world. Her miner's cabin became my bubble. However, the real question was, *"who was going to protect me from grandma?"*

I could go on and on for days about this funeral-going Grandma with her stage name. It would be difficult to quantify what I gained from her, as it is an infinite collection of minutia – we need to save every piece of string and wire for future use; we listened to the "Grand Ole Opry" on Saturday night while she made finger shadow puppets on the walls of the cabin as I fell asleep; we made fudge from scratch on a wood stove. Above all, Grandma Bett told me over and over again, that of all the bad things that can happen to a person during their lifetime, the worst thing, by far, was war. I have not forgotten that valuable lesson, and I do believe that she was right.

She paid $50 in the 1930's for a used, but good quality, upright piano and had it moved into the two room miner's cabin so her children could learn to play, as she was certain that this would make them cultured. I eventually inherited the piano but never mastered playing it, nor did my Dad, nor my Aunt. When I sold the piano last year, it took four men to lift it into the horse trailer used to move it back to the John Christian family in Pioche, the descendents of the original owner. Now maybe one of their children or grandchildren will become cultured!

The Pioche miner's cabin was about 15' X 20' with one wall down the middle dividing the space into two rooms. One room had a wood burning stove, cold running water with one spigot directing the water into a large metal sink, one wooden table for dining, and a single bed where my dad had slept when he lived there. In the other room was a double bed for Grandma and her daughter, my Aunt

Kathryn, one rocker, a dresser, and the immensely heavy upright piano.

There was no bathroom plumbing in this miner's cabin, which was the norm. The outhouse was— well, outside, and with Pioche perched on the side of two mountains at an elevation of 5,200 feet, it could be very cold in the winter. The cabin had no insulation and no drywall. The best the little family could do was to paper the walls with newspapers to mitigate the effects of the north wind. Thank goodness for the wood stove. It did its duty in keeping the place warm enough to support survival.

These were the living conditions for almost every mining family in the United States up to the 1940s. Only mining executives and maybe superintendents lived in larger traditional houses. Miners and their families came and went in these camps, and 15' X 20' miner's cabins were the production homes in every mining camp in the West. When looking on-line for information about the dimensions of these cabins, I found, much to my amazement, that they are being offered as vacation rentals in areas like the gold country of California at $40 per night....Oh my goodness – nostalgia just won't take me that far!

Am I like this grandma? Probably a bit more than I would really like to admit! I loved these three grandparents equally, and I loved them each deeply. I was so lucky to be able to engage with all three in very intimate settings – never doing exciting things like going to Disneyland, but just accompanying them on their daily activities – that's where the real learning about life occurs.

Yet, there was always the phantom grandfather who died before I was born, hovering in the ether above me. His children were ages 10 and 12 when he died. What was he like? Is it possible that I am more like him than the other three? Would I have liked him? Would he have liked me?

These re-occurring thoughts and feelings finally spurred me into action. I realized that in order to satisfy my curiosity about this grandpa, I needed to dig into my family records and any other resources that I could come by to put together a picture of this man. Of course, it would have been better if I had come to this conclusion prior to the passing of my Dad and my Aunt; but, better late than never. This investigation has led me to some very interesting places, and I think Grandpa would be proud to share his history with all of us.

Grandpa Becomes a Tramp Miner

Roscoe Hamilton Wilkes, was born at Round Grove, Missouri, on May 14, 1877. Round Grove is about halfway between Joplin and Springfield. He was the son of Richard Porter Wilkes and Nancy Catherine Wooley who owned a small farm and a very small country store. Richard and Nancy had four children, Roscoe, Maude, Gertrude and Bessie. Nancy died in 1886, one year after the birth of Bessie, leaving Richard alone with four youngsters. Within several years he re-married Elizabeth Hauger, who raised his four children and gave birth to five more, Harry, Ruth, Blanche, Mamie and Richard Jr.

Both of Roscoe's grandparents were born in Lawrence County, Missouri, as well, and the Wilkes family tree can be traced back to early colonists, Minor Wilkes born 1735, Samuel Snead born 1720, Richard Straughan born 1732, John Brownlow born 1724 and William Saunders born 1740. The Joplin/Springfield area is located in southwest Missouri, a short distance from the Missouri-Arkansas border, which was the "Mason-Dixon Line" established during the Civil War, dividing the Northern from the Southern states. Both of Roscoe's grandfathers, Carroll Wooley and Richard S. Wilkes, served in the Missouri Militia during the Civil War.

By the time Roscoe was 16, which would have been 1893, the small farm was over-crowded with this large brood, and his father was struggling to feed nine children with the income from the small farm and country store. Roscoe, the oldest, and now close to a full grown man, was encouraged to lend a hand to an uncle who owned a ranch in Wyoming. Out of the nine siblings, six were girls, leaving Richard Porter

Wilkes with very few options but to encourage the boys to go out on their own as soon as they were old enough.

Roscoe took the only opportunity offered and left for Wyoming, where he quickly morphed from a Missouri sapling into a bonafide Wyoming cowboy. I'm not sure if he liked ranch life, but I am positive that he loved the wide open spaces of the West, as he only returned to Missouri for short visits—seemingly to court and to marry young women closely connected with his large family.

I was unable to find any trace of Grandpa from 1893 until 1904. We have several pictures of him riding bucking horses in a corral adjacent to ranch out-buildings with a wide open prairie vista in the distance. I'm supposing that these photos were taken on his uncle's Wyoming ranch. The next spotting of Roscoe is a listing for him in the 1904 Pueblo, Colorado, city directory. There were no telephones listed, but the directory was published with all of its citizen's addresses and occupations. He was listed as a teamster residing at 1424 Palmer Avenue, and in 1905, he had moved to 618 W. 7th St.

Teamsters around the turn of the century drove a team of horses 12 to 18 hours per day, seven days a week, for $2.00 per day; and we wonder how the unions got started and became so powerful— the answer being, *"out of the desperation of millions of men driving team every waking hour in order to feed their families."*

Pueblo, Colorado, is located 112 miles due south of Denver at the confluence of the Arkansas River and Fountain Creek. It sits at an elevation of 4,692 feet and currently boasts a population of 106,000. Although situated at a fairly high altitude, it is located in a semi-arid high desert, known as the banana belt of Colorado, providing Pueblo citizens a very livable climate.

It is still today one of the largest steel producing cities in the U.S. At the turn of the century the population was already 28,000 and grew to 42,000 by 1920. Due to the rapid growth of the steel mills, employment skyrocketed during this period attracting multitudes of immigrant laborers, including Irish, Italian, German, Slovenian, Greek, Jewish, Lithuanian, Russian, Hungarian, Japanese and African Americans. At one point, 40 different languages were being spoken in the steel mills, and as a result, Pueblo became, and still is, a very cosmopolitan town.

Now this seems to me to be a perfect place for an up-and-coming, industrious young man from Missouri to put down roots and prosper; but this story takes a left turn at this point. We lose the trail of Roscoe until the census of 1910, where he is listed as residing in Keensbury, Colorado, a very small town in northeastern Colorado, with Lena Bowles, then age 30, and her 23-year-old sister. Lena is listed as a *"hotel keeper"* and Roscoe is listed as a *"pool hall manager."* Lena Bowles was born officially as Elena Bowles in 1881, at Round Grove, Missouri, the same little fork in the road as our Roscoe. He was four years her senior, but must have grown up with her. To complicate things, records show that Elena Bowles married Frank Oliver Walker, a farmer, in 1905, and gave birth to a daughter in 1906.

Somehow, between 1906 and 1910, Elena had divorced Frank Walker, and married grandpa! I was never able to locate a marriage certificate for Elena and Roscoe, but did find a divorce decree for them; so they were, in fact, legally married sometime between 1906 and the 1910 census.

The next sighting of grandpa is in 1914, where he and Lena appear in the Denver, Colorado, city directory as renting a room at 1343 Stout St. Somehow between the 1910 census and 1914, it appears that Roscoe had left his career as a pool hall manager and had taken up the profession of mining. We know this because, in January of 1914, he signed a contract with the Braden Copper Co. of Montana to ship out to South America (Chile) to work for a year as a machinist at the El Teniente Copper mine near Sewell, Chile. Sewell is located in the Andes, 52 miles south of Santiago. He had to have had a documentable work history in mining by that time to be able to qualify for this contract. However, to date, I have not been able to establish his whereabouts between 1910 and 1914.

Trampin' in, pard? Roscoe Wilkes was not only a miner, but was a full-fledged tramp miner by 1914. Lena did not go with him on this assignment. We will never know if the assignment in Chile caused them to part, or, if they would have parted regardless, and Roscoe decided to take the assignment because of this break up. But, we do know— proof positive— that he returned on Jan. 26, 1915, through the port at New Orleans.

Roscoe Hamilton Wilkes is listed as one of 16 passengers in the manifest of the ship, S.S. Parismina, which sailed from Colon, (Cristobal, C.Z.) which was Panama, on January 21, 1915, arriving at the Port of New Orleans on January 26, 1915. The 16 passengers showed U.S. addresses all over the country from New Jersey to Oakland, California, and even Bohemia.

The S.S. Parismina was built in 1908 for Tropical Fruit S.S. Co., Ltd. It was a steam ship designed mostly for cargo and a few passengers – 120ft. X 15.2 ft. Later it was purchased by the U.S. Navy and was torpedoed in 1942 by a German sub on a trip from Reykjavik to Boston.

I was unable to find a ship's manifest to document Roscoe's trip to Chile, but I am assuming that he travelled there by the same route that he used for return. Many of the miners travelling to mines in South America were sent on similar steam ships out of San Francisco and travelled south along the pacific coast to their destinations in Peru, Bolivia, Columbia and Chile – all countries with large mines— many owned by U.S. corporations. The geology of the Andes Mountains is similar to the Rockies in the U.S. and was rich with many of the same minerals as were being mined in the North American Rocky Mountains and the Sierra Nevada's.

Since Roscoe was currently residing in Denver and still had family in Missouri, it may have been less expensive to route him from New Orleans. He would have continued through the Panama Canal to the Pacific Ocean travelling down the west coast of South America to Santiago, Chile. We do have photos that he had labeled "Peru;" "La Paz, Bolivia;" as well as "Molino, Chile;" and photos of the Braden Copper Company where he was employed. Since he had signed a year's contract, and the U.S. workers were generally not allowed much vacation by the employers, he might have made stops in these other countries, as the transport ship stopped to load or unload cargo at their ports of call.

It seemed that the miners of this era had an excellent "word-of-mouth" rumor mill and were making friends and staying in touch through letters and messages sent via acquaintances. One picture in Peru of two very well dressed American men and one woman was labeled "*friends in Peru*." How did Grandpa make these friends? How did he stay in touch with them? Where in Peru were they? I have followed every possible clue I could think of to answer these questions, but have come up empty handed.

The short of it is that my grandfather had become an adventurer, and he was no longer bound by borders. He was a tramp miner, and tramp miners went without trepidation to where-ever the next opportunity led them, and they made friends along the way. Fellow travelers always bond quickly.

El Teniente Mine, Chile

William Braden, the owner of Braden Copper Co. was a graduate of MIT and began his career in Montana. He was first sent to Chile by his employer in 1894 to explore mining possibilities. On a subsequent trip in 1903, an Italian mining engineer by the name of Chiapponi was scouting for mines with Braden and called his attention to an abandoned mine known as "*El Teniente*," which means "*the lieutenant*" in Spanish. Several rich deposits had been worked in prior eras, but other nationalities had turned it down in recent years, determining that the ore was not rich enough to warrant improvements.

Braden got the idea of mining it as a huge mass of low grade copper – not much more than 2%— which had not been done anywhere in the world up to that time. While surveying the vista from a nearby mountain top, he discovered that this low grade concentrate ran around the entire rim of an extinct volcano. No other prospectors or geologists had evaluated the whole of it in this manner.

William Braden, with his own money and that of several partners, created the Braden Copper Company. The challenges in making this operation viable were many. The mine was located at 6,000 feet and was in a central valley which became heavily snow-laden in the winters, with snow drifts reaching 50 feet – totally unappealing to Chilean miners. Braden had to operate 365 days per year to make this mine pay due to the challenge of mining low-grade ore. His challenge was how to put together a work force of miners who were adamantly averse to working in those conditions?

Braden was not just an average MIT graduate. He had creative business sense as well as technical expertise. He made placards showing a *"Horn of Plenty"* over-flowing with gold and placed the placards near every mine in Chile, advertising a lottery with handsome prizes. Every miner signing a contract in the autumn (our spring) and staying until September would receive free tickets for the lottery – and, by golly, it worked!

Braden kept the wages at the El Teniente the highest in Chile; he built snug frame boarding houses for all employees; he provided free schooling; and sold household items at the company store below wholesale. On the flip side, no liquor was permitted at the mines and this was strictly enforced. The Chilean miners – known to be really big drinkers – had no choice but to stay sober at the El Teniente. However, it is rumored that more than one run was made on foot over the steep Andes by eager distributors delivering liquor to the well-paid miners.

The challenges kept coming one after another, as happens with most ambitious projects – challenges in bringing in enough timber; financial challenges with the bond holders, the Guggenheims—and on and on. However, in the end, the Braden Copper Company contributed greatly to the national wealth of Chile for generations; they raised the bar for the living conditions of the Chilean workers; and they produced the lion's share of the copper required by the United States for the war effort during World War I and World War II.

Kennecott Copper Company purchased the mine in 1915, and the El Teniente survives today as a division of *"Codelco,"* remaining the world's largest underground copper mine. I believe that my grandfather's contract was with Braden Copper Company, as it was signed in January of 1915, right before Braden sold to Kennecott.

Roscoe's passport shows that he was hired to be a machinist, and most likely did not work underground. There were plenty of Chilean miners for the underground jobs, but it was difficult to find engineers and metallurgists and skilled workers for the U.S. machinery that was being developed for the South American mines – they were all being imported.

I spoke recently to John Gomes, who graduated in mining engineering from the Mackey School of Mines at U.N.R. in 1950. Directly out of college, he took a job in Peru at the Sierra De Pasco mine as a junior metallurgist, joining the ranks of the tramp miners of old. The mine was located at 13,000 feet causing altitude sickness for some of the American workers, including Gomes. He reported that the living conditions for the Americans were dormitory style and decent. However, the Peruvian miners lived in large barracks with no running water – just one spigot out in the yard for many workers, and they were making $4.00 per day. Gomes was forced to return home after several months due to the altitude sickness. Trampin' in to South America isn't for everyone.

Roscoe Sr. Becomes a Family Man

Roscoe Wilkes was back in the U.S. in January of 1915, after his exciting adventure in South America. I imagine that he returned to Colorado, but his year's absence did not bode well for his marriage to Lena Bowles Wilkes, as they were divorced in Weld County, Colorado, on June 22, 1915. They had no children. This is the same county where Roscoe and Lena operated the hotel and pool hall. It is also where Lena's ex-husband, Frank Walker, was living. It appears that Lena went back to Frank, and the two of them subsequently moved to southern California where they lived together until their deaths.

I believe that Roscoe was mining in Colorado for the next few years. There is a post card from a resort outside of Salt Lake City, known as "Saltaire," dated 1917, showing bathers relaxing in the salt waters of the Great Salt Lake. This would have been a likely vacation spot for a divorced, Colorado miner flush with bonus money from South America.

The next documented date noting Roscoe's whereabouts is March 1, 1917, when he signed a contract with the Platinum Mining and Milling Co. of Wyoming, known as the "Rambler Mine." My grandmother had saved this contract. The contract is four pages long and is signed by the general manager, Dorchester Mapes. Interesting excerpts from the contract are as follows:

"THE COMPANY agrees to employ and does hereby employ the said ROSCOE H. WILKES to act as and to perform the duties of General Superintendent of the mining property, now being operated by

THE COMPANY and known as the RAMBLER MINE, situated in Albany County, Wyoming.....

"It is the essence of this agreement that THE COMPANY'S affairs shall, in all ways, be so conducted as to reflect no discredit upon THE COMPANY and its property so operated as to develop the mine in a miner-like fashion and with a view to placing and maintaining it on a profit-producing basis without sacrificing or jeopardizing future profitable operations.....

"THE SUPERINTENDENT is to have full power to hire and discharge employees of all classes and for all work necessary to the carrying out of the conditions hereof...."

"THE SUPERINTENDENT shall govern himself and all the men in THE COMPANY'S employ, under him, in strict compliance with the Wyoming State Law with respect to the use of Intoxicating Liquor, which law reads as follows, to wit:

"Whoever shall, while under the influence of intoxicating liquor, enter any mine, smelter or metallurgical works or any of the buildings connected with the operation of the same in Wyoming, where miners or other workmen are employed, or carry any intoxicating liquor into the same, shall be deemed guilty of a misdemeanor, and upon conviction, shall be fined in any sum not exceeding five hundred dollars, to which may be added imprisonment in the county jail for a term not exceeding one year. And any violation of this law by any employee of THE COMPANY shall be considered cause for immediate discharge."....

"THE SUPERINTENDENT is to be allowed a vacation of one month, on half pay. THE COMPANY is to furnish and provide THE SUPERINTENDENT, during the period of actual service herunder, with room and with board at THE COMPANY'S regular boarding house, while at the mine and is to pay all of his legitimate and reasonable traveling expenses, including.....

THE COMPANY agrees to pay to THE SUPERINTENDENT, in consideration for the faithful performance of the conditions hereof the sum of Two Hundred Dollars ($200.00) per month from March 1st, 1917, to August 31st., 1917 and the sum of Two Hundred and Twenty Five Dollars ($250.00) per month from September 1st, 1917, to February, 28th, 1918.

THIS AGREEMENT shall be and remain in force for a period of one year from the date herof, unless, for some reason, now unforeseen, it becomes impossible or impracticable to continue operations, in which case THE COMPANY *may terminate the agreement by paying to* THE SUPERINTENDENT *a sum equal to two month's salary in addition to full salary up to the date operations are discontinued...."*

With the good news of this prestigious contract, my grandfather travelled within the next 60 days to Missouri and married my grandmother, Estella Maud Neal, in Joplin, Missouri, on May 10, 1917. He was four days short of turning 40 years old, and Estella Maud was 26. Their respective families had lived for several generations in Missouri counties that were located adjacent to one another. My dad also recalled that at some time prior to this, a small boy in the Wilkes family had been orphaned and taken in by a relative of my grandmother's (in the Neal family.) Roscoe and Maud had to have known one another or at least known of one another for years, but we have no letters to confirm this, or anything pertaining to their courtship. I do know my grandmother would have been elated to marry this handsome Missouri gentleman turned world-traveler, who showed such promise for the future in the mining industry.

The Rambler mine, located in the southern Rocky Mountains, was discovered in 1877. It is due west of Laramie, Wyoming, in Albany County in the northern section of the Medicine Bow National Forest. The mine was situated at an elevation of 9,700 feet. The ore was 11% copper associated with palladium, platinum, gold and silver. The mine's records show that they were mining seven to ten tons of ore daily in 1917. However, the records also show that from Aug. 16, 1916, to March 1917, their income from ore sales was $3,351, and the income from stock sales was $16,200. Their expenditures were $22,648. When a mine is making more from the sale of stock than from the sale of its mineral product, the future of that mine is very questionable.

Shortly after my grandfather signed the contract, the Rambler mine suffered a raging fire and was shut down—it was not re-opened for many years. Such are the vagaries of the mining industry. This beautiful, mountainous area in the Medicine Bow National Forest is now dotted with Wyoming vacation homes.

Tramp Mining With Babies

I was not able to find out the exact date of the fire and closing of the Rambler mine, but within months of his marriage, Roscoe was forced into relocating – this time not by choice. My grandmother had saved her wedding book, signed by everyone at the wedding, which also contained some family information added by her at later dates. On one small extra page provided for written "congratulations" by guests, Grandma had documented many of the places they lived during their marriage, and the places appear to be in chronological order.

The first place listed is the Rambler Mine in Holmes, Wyoming (May 1917). The wedding book is also signed by Dorchester and Edna Mapes, the General Manager of the Rambler mine who had signed the contract. Also, Grandma lists a short stop in Rawlins, Wyoming. The fire and closing of the mine had to have occurred sometime after the newly married couple arrived in Wyoming for Roscoe to report to work. Then, to further complicate their lives, the newly-weds would soon discover that Estella Maud was with child.

The next documented work place for Roscoe is Mescada, Sonora, Mexico. He later lists on an application for a passport that he had resided in Mescada, Mexico from Oct. 28, 1917 until Dec. 17, 1917. Undoubtedly, Grandma returned to her family in Burns, Missouri, to await the birth of her child, when her husband took this 60 day job in Mexico. Her child, Roscoe Harold, was born January 25, 1918, in Burns, Missouri.

Roscoe probably left Mexico (Sonora is in northwestern Mexico, and the mine may have been close to the U.S.

boarder) returning to Burns for the holidays and to wait for the baby to be born. There were established train lines running from Phoenix to St. Louis, Missouri by that time. Within seven weeks of the birth, on March 14, 1918, the couple packed up their newborn son and left the U.S. en route to Cananea, Sonora, Mexico – a different mine in Sonora. They remained at Cananea until November, as they both applied for passports at that time, with Roscoe listing his occupation as Shift Boss of the Cananea Consolidated Copper Co. The passports were issued on Jan. 6, 1919.

Passports had not been required of U.S. citizens, except by executive order, which had been enforced during the Civil War and during World War 1 from 1914 through 1918. The law requiring that all citizens must have a passport to leave and return to the U.S. was passed on Nov. 29, 1941. I believe that during World War I, men could leave and return to the U.S. without a passport, if they could produce an employment contract, especially for mining, in another country. Mining would often warrant an exemption from serving in the military.

Roscoe is described in the passport as being 5' 11" tall and clean shaven, with gray hair, square chin, a Roman nose and blue eyes. Estella Maud is described in her passport as 5' 6" with dark brown hair and grey eyes. The passport states that she is accompanied by her minor child, Roscoe Harold, and the passport picture shows mother holding her baby.

The copper mine at Cananea is one of the oldest copper mines on the North American continent, operating since 1899, and had one of the largest reserves of copper in the world. The mine was in operation until June of 2007, when the miners went on strike for better working conditions, striking against the owner, Grupo Mexico. Grupo evidently broke the strike, but the mine has remained closed since that time.

By late summer of 1919, the couple would have realized that Maud was expecting their second child. They may have tired of living in Mexico. We don't know exactly when they returned stateside, but Maud lists in her wedding book, Ouray, Colorado, on a line between Cananea, Mexico, and Phoenix, Az. Kathryn Aileen, baby sister, as she was always referred to by her parents, was born Feb. 13, 1920, in Prescott, Arizona, and her daddy was listed as a "shift boss" at the Blue Bell Mine outside of Mayer, Arizona.

I found one postcard written in my grandmother's hand dated July 18, 1920, from Pueblo, Colorado, saying:

Dear Daddy,
I am tired. Will get out 1:30 and get home Tuesday eve. Will write as soon as I get there.
Yours,
Maud

This postcard is addressed to R.H. Wilkes, Sunnyside Mine, Eureka, Colorado. Had they left Arizona already?

Since she is saying she will write when she gets home, she is not on her way to join him. It appears to me that she was going back to her relatives in Missouri again for a time until her husband was able to get settled in the new job and find a place to live. She would have been on the train with a four-month old baby and a two-and-a-half year old toddler—no wonder she is tired! Neither of them knew it then, but this was to be the new norm for their lives for the next eight years.

The best I can piece together from photographs, memorabilia, letters and the wedding book, their movements are as follows:

1912/1920—Christmas in Silverton, Colorado—Roscoe employed at the "Sunnyside mine"

1920 or 1921—Mack, Colorado – 10 miles east of Utah boarder.

1921—Telluride, Colorado

1921 or 1922—Silverton, Colorado

1921 or 1922—Salida, Colorado

1/24/1924—Silverton, Colorado—(Quite a few family pictures at this time in Silverton with parents and children looking well dressed – reflection of a good job.

Letter from Roscoe to his son, Roscoe Harold:

> *"Eureka, Colorado*
> *Jan. 24, 1924*
> *Mr. R. H. Wilkes, Jr.*
>
> *Dear Son – As tomorrow is your Birthday and you are Six years old I am sending you a Present – so I thought – one dollar for each year would be about right –*
> *When a boy is Six years old it is a good time to start a Bank Account – so find Enclosed $6.00 and*
> *Best Wishes from your Daddy,*
>
> *R. H. Wilkes, Sr.*
>
> *Tell sister I will send her a Present when she is four years old."*

1924—Pioche, Nevada

I have to believe that Roscoe Sr. did work for a short period of time in the Combined Metals Number 1 mine, but any records to prove this would be impossible to find. On the way to Pioche, the family stopped in Las Vegas for several weeks and rented a small house on east Fremont St. while Roscoe looked around.

Roscoe Harold, then about six years old, had left Colorado with a sizeable collection of what he felt were very valuable marbles, and he fancied himself as an ace marble player. Over the course of a week he lost every marble to the neighborhood Las Vegas boys. My grandmother told Roscoe Sr.,

> *"It wasn't his fault. That boy that won all the marbles is the son of a professional gambler."*

1926—Grand Junction, Colorado—Wilkes Beauty Shop (Maud had gone into business as a hairdresser.)

10/1926—3/1927—Red Cliff and Palisade, Colorado—(Maud ran a country store). The dates above are the dates listed on Roscoe Harold's report card in Red Cliff.

My Dad often told the story that Daddy would leave and go to another town to find a better job. The family would then wait for him to send a letter or telegraph that he had living quarters arranged, and they were to follow. Then, Maud and the two children would pack up and board the next train with their suitcases and a big basket of fried chicken and baking powder biscuits—they were off with high hopes and dreams to join Daddy in the next town—only to repeat the process again in six months or less.

My Dad remembers spending a great deal of time hanging out the windows of many trains, which he really enjoyed. His mother was always hollering at him to get his head back inside the train so he wouldn't get a cinder in his eye. Of course this fell on deaf ears, and he would be plagued for miles of train travel while his mother tried to wash out the most recent cinder.

If I had written this book when my dad, Roscoe Jr., was still alive, the detail would have been better; but, like many things in life, it just didn't happen. In short, this little family who started out with the same vision of every family in the

United States to live the American dream, had become a family of migrant workers with a deteriorating life style, and with children who were being moved from school to school sometimes twice in one year.

The back-story is that by the time the second child was born, Roscoe Sr. was 43—older for a hard rock miner. A shift boss or superintendent can work much longer. However, Roscoe Sr. was losing his hearing, undoubtedly from the blasting when he was underground and from the noise of the machinery above ground—the noise from the stamps (crushers) was deafening.

I talked to the curator, Casey Carroll, at the mining museum in Silverton, Colorado—which, by the way, is an excellent small museum with wonderful underground exhibits. She told me that all of the old men in Silverton are deaf – that it is taken for granted in restaurants and other public places that men over a certain age are going to be stone deaf. Back then, there were no disability benefits for miners. Actually, there were no disability benefits for anyone until Congress passed that addition to the Social Security Act in 1956.

The Wilkes children grew up feeling like their dad was a rolling stone, and they felt abandoned because he left so often. After spending months with the research for this book, I have come away with a different feeling. My Dad did tell me that at a certain point the kids had to yell into a long horn to communicate with their father— that says a lot— this, and the fact that he was working on and off as a barber and Maud was working when she could as a beautician, tells me that Roscoe Sr. was struggling with a serious disability beyond his control.

Coasting into Pioche

In 1927, Roscoe Sr. and Maud, who by this time was answering to Betty, once again loaded up the kids and their belongings into their Dodge Touring car with isinglass curtains and headed for Oregon. I do not know what Roscoe Sr. had planned for Oregon – he was definitely a man of many plans—but they took off from Colorado on a Friday after school, arriving in Pioche, Nevada on a Sunday.

On the high road just a few miles outside of Pioche, the Dodge Touring car started knocking. They made it to the top of Main Street, just below the entrance to the Number 1 mine, and then coasted into town. Roscoe pulled into a parking place in front of the Pioche barbershop. That was the end of the Dodge Touring car, as it had thrown a rod, and the end to the plans for Oregon. My aunt recalls that Roscoe Jr. jumped out of the car and started dancing in the street. They had been in Pioche a few years previously, and the kids had made good friends. It had been the happiest of the many stopping places for the children, and they had fond memories of Pioche.

My aunt Kathryn writes:

> *"Sunday became a day of action. Dad discussed work possibilities; Maud found a house to rent, and we moved in. On Monday morning my brother and I were back in school. This stop-over became a lengthy one, lasting for many years. The Oregon move never became a reality."*

I believe that by this time, Roscoe's hearing was too far gone for him to get a job at any of the local mines. Hearing is absolutely a necessity underground, and even above ground, you have to be able to hear. Mines, under-ground as well as above-ground are dangerous places, and no one wants to work with an impaired colleague in this environment. Therefore, I think according to my dad, Roscoe went to work in the barbershop on Main Street.

With all of the moves and the stress of a husband who was struggling to make a living, my grandparent's marriage was coming apart at the seams. I recently read Wallace Stegner's book, "*Angle of Repose.*" It is a work of fiction but based on the letters of Mary Hallock Foote, a famous east coast magazine illustrator of the late 1800's, who married a mining engineer and ended up living her life in mining camps of the West, and I quote,

> "*She saw in his face that he had contracted the incurable Western disease. He had set his cross-hairs on the snowpeak of a vision, and there he would go, triangulating his way across a bone-dry future, dragging her and the children with him, until they all died of thirst.*"

Stegman summed up the whole existence of tramp miners and their families in two well thought-out sentences. The Wilkes family was dying of thirst. The father was desperate to make a living for his wife and two children and kept visualizing a mirage in the distance – a new town, and a new mine that would offer him a better job, and he continued to chase the mirage.

The mother was suffering from not enough money to buy the food and clothing needed for these two growing children, from being left alone for weeks on end with all of the problems of the children, and from the loss of social status when her husband's career started down a fast decline. In addition, these two healthy, attractive and smart kids were getting moved from school to school, sometimes twice or more in one grade – forever leaving friends behind, missing their father, always being the new kid on the block, and in some cases not being acknowledged by their teachers, as they were the disposable children of a tramp-miner and would be gone soon anyway.

Looking at the family photo album, I see lots of pictures of the kids as babies and up to the stop at Silverton, Colorado in 1924. The parents and children both look well-dressed in attractive, well-fitting clothing. After 1924, there are almost no photos.

So, in the summer of 1928, Roscoe Sr. had once again left his family in Pioche and found his way to Tybo, Nevada, the latest boom town, hoping for better work than what he was getting in Pioche.

In 1876, Tybo had been a typical Nevada mining boom town boasting a population of 1,000, but with 100 people remaining after the mine folded in 1881. The town boomed again in 1916 and in 1926, when new mining companies began working the mines, building new mills and housing. The rush was over by 1937, and the mines were never worked again – only mining tailings and the ruins of a few buildings remain.

The letter Roscoe wrote to his wife and kids on August 27, 1928, does not sound to me in any way like a man who was planning on leaving his wife and children. He sounds optimistic – like he probably always sounded when writing from the latest boom town. Unfortunately, however, this is the last communication I could find from Roscoe Sr. According to my Aunt and my Dad, the couple separated, and Roscoe returned to Pueblo, Colorado.

Reading between the lines, I think it is reasonable to assume that he was not able to get a full time position in Tybo and was not able to send money to Bett, as she was now known in Pioche. I believe that Grandma could not take any more disappointments from Roscoe Sr. and sent him packing – her decision, not his.

He returned to Pueblo, Colorado, to the Wilkes barbershop. He suffered a massive heart attack on June 9, 1930, and died. His family in Missouri retrieved his body and had him buried in Verona, Missouri, in the Wilkes family plot.

Bett wrote one last entry in her wedding book, *"Daddy Wilkes gone June 1930."* She obviously loved this man, but the problems of life with him had become more than she could cope with. The disappointment that he was bringing to the family may have been more than he could cope with, as well.

Everyone Was Poor

Roscoe Jr. was now 12 and Kathryn Aileen, was 10. Pioche was just like all of the other mining camps where they had lived in almost every way but one. The kids had made friends on the prior trip—about three years earlier—with the Franks family. Their parents had also divorced, and their father had left the area. Danny and John Franks were close to Roscoe Jr.'s age, and their sister, Dolly, was the same age as Kathryn. Dolly and Kathryn even looked alike, and many of the town's people could not tell one from the other. The five of them took up immediately where they had left off three years previously and remained the best of friends until the end of their lives. It was a connection that probably saved the sanity of all five children and their respective mothers, as well.

Most people were poor in Pioche—it was the beginning of the depression. The town was even more remote than the towns in Colorado, which perhaps forced the citizens to stick together for survival. The kids ran in bunches, and folks tried to look after the widows and their offspring.

Grandma continued to style hair. My Dad carried ice and wood for various people in town – including the house of ill repute, where the reigning madam would tip him liberally and invite him in for a large piece of cake after every delivery. The farmers from Panaca would give my grandmother extra produce left on the trucks at the end of their deliveries.

Eventually, when Roscoe Jr. turned age 14, he got a job as the night telephone operator – there weren't too many phone calls at night, so he was able to do his homework and sleep at the telephone office. He held this job through high school. They lived on dried beans, potatoes and biscuits for the most part, which were stored under the single bed in the two room miner's cabin. The Wilkes kids were treated equally in the school system and both excelled scholastically and in the extra- curricular activities that were offered. My Aunt writes at her age 80:

> *"Maud guided us thru grammar school, a period of youthful adventures, and into the formative high school years. I especially liked the depression. All Dads were out of work; all families felt hardships. I knew we would be poor without the depression, but I had company. Maud made my prom dress out of blue and white dotted swiss, and it was beautiful as I paraded proudly with the royalty as first attendant."*

Bett emphasized education to her two children with every opportunity, repeating over and over that they needed to go to college and become teachers. That was her answer to over-coming poverty. When Roscoe Jr. became a senior in High School he realized that the only way he could afford college tuition was to get a job underground at the Number 1 mine in Pioche for at least the summer months prior to leaving for college.

He walked to the mine every morning for an hour before school for six weeks straight and stood in line with the other miners looking for work that day. He was passed over week after week. Low and behold, the day after school let out, the foreman waived him over from the line and said, *"You can go to work."* Those five words changed the course of history for the Roscoe Wilkes family.

Since Roscoe Jr. was under the age of 18, he needed his mother's signature to go underground. His mother had refused for months to sign the paper – she did not want him underground under any circumstances, as she had lived in enough mining camps to fully understand the significance of working in the hole. Finally, Roscoe Jr. convinced her that it was the only way he could better himself. She signed the paper with tears running down her cheeks. The management at the Number 1 mine was watching out for this disadvantaged young man and kept him working until September. Roscoe was off to Spearfish Teacher's college where he earned a two-year teaching degree, returning to Pioche in two years to take his first teaching job in Carp, Nevada.

Kathryn graduated from Lincoln County High School two years after her brother and left for the University of Nevada at Reno, where she worked and took classes until she had earned a four year degree in English Literature and Business. She taught English for over 30 years in various Nevada high schools, mainly at Lincoln County High School—her alma mater—serving the next generation of miners and their children.

It pains me to think that Roscoe Sr. left Nevada a broken man— unable to hear; having trouble finding a job to feed his family; losing the confidence of his wife; and finally retreating to Pueblo, Colorado by himself; ultimately succumbing to a heart attack at age 53. He had no way of knowing what a success his two children would make of their lives.

Roscoe Jr. enlisted in the Army Air Corp in World War II and became an officer, survived a Romanian prison camp, and then attended USC Law School on the G.I. Bill. He was elected District Attorney in Lincoln County (Pioche is the county seat), was appointed District Judge in Lincoln and White Pine County, and finally was appointed as an Administrative Law judge for the Coast Guard in Seattle. Oh, if his father could have lived to see all of this!

Kathryn lived to age 90, enjoying a wonderful teaching career and long marriage to Press (Bud) Duffin. They had one daughter, Mary Kathryn Stasak. Roscoe lived to age 95, outliving his first wife, Alberta Viney Wilkes, and his second wife, Lois Wilkes. He and Bertie had two daughters, Karen Wilkes Martin (me) and Stephanie Cumings, one granddaughter, Kayla Cumings, and one great-grandson, Dysen Fass.

In writing this story, I have come to a new and deeper understanding of who my grandfather was. Am I more like him than the other grandparents? Well, I don't know for sure, but there are several traits that we seem to share. It appears to me that he was definitely a cock-eyed optimist – always sure that the next stop was going to be the best, and my glass is generally half full or more. And, I really love to travel – say *"airplane"* and I'm packing a suitcase.

So, it came to me one day, half way through writing this story, that I should share a trip with my grandfather. The only way I could figure out how to do this was to follow his steps. I had already been to the Blue Bell mine in Mayer, Az.—what fun that was, except for the hair-raising ride down the mountain on a very washed-out and remote dirt road. I had also been to Silverton, Colorado, and surrounding towns with my husband several years ago. The road from Silverton to Durango is unbelievably nerve-racking, even today—I can't imagine traveling on it in the 1920's. I also grew up a half mile from the Number 1 mine in Pioche. What part of my grandfather's journey is left for me to experience? Well, how about The El Teniente mine in Chile?

Following Grandpa's Steps to Chile

Say no more. It's July 21, 2016, and I am off to the nearest travel agent to plan my trip to Chile. Grandpa, I know you would be proud of me and would surely hop on board if you could. I'm convinced that I will feel your presence on this trip, and maybe I will completely figure you out. Stay tuned!

1:27 P.M.—October 20, 2016—Darryl and I fasten our seat-belts, push our carry-ons under the seat in front of us and prepare for takeoff. Delta DL817 revs its engines, and we look at each other with knowing grins. We're off to Atlanta where we have two hours to transfer to the international terminal and board our ten hour flight to Santiago, Chile—yes, it's really a long way down to Chile, close to 5,000 miles—the size of the South American continent had never really registered with me until now—it's huge!

10:27 P.M.—preparing to take off with a fully loaded plane to Santiago – many of the passengers dressed in REI clothing, boots and puffer coats and jackets. The guide book had mentioned that Santiago is the jumping off place for travelers on their way to Patagonia.

8:55 A.M.—October 21st—Prepare for landing in Santiago – long night—too excited to sleep—too excited to read—worked on cross word puzzle most of the night—easy moving through Customs—supposed to be met by an English speaking guide and driver—I'm skeptical about this. Wow! There's a young man holding up a sign that says

"Wilkes"—how about that! We are taken to meet our driver, Catalina, and we're off to the city and to the Atton Hotel—so far, so good.

Exhaustion is setting in, but our room is ready and a nap is possible – whew! Later in the afternoon we explore the area around the hotel, enjoy some Chilean cuisine (warm empanadas), and settle down for a good night's rest, as tomorrow we embark on our journey to the El Teniente Copper mine, where Grampa, Roscoe Hamilton Wilkes, mined in 1914. I can't believe this is really happening!

7:30 A.M.,—Oct. 22nd—Catalina meets us promptly in front of the Hotel and drives us to meet the "Sewell" tour bus. Sewell, Chile, is the village that was built by the Braden Copper Co. for management and employees at the El Teniente mine, and is now a Unesco World Heritage site.

El Teniente is the largest underground mine in the world with 1,491 miles of tunnels which yield 440,000 tons of refined copper per year. The village of Sewell was a residentially segregated community – not segregated by race, but by classes of job descriptions, with the North American managers occupying the most comfortable residences, then the North American technicians, which would have been my grandfather and others, the Chilean support staff, and lastly, a mass of Chilean miners.

8:25 A.M.—It's a crisp clear day—as clear as Santiago can be with its thousands of Chinese made cars sans catalytic converters lining the streets—as we settle on the Sewell tour bus with about twenty other tourists – six of us speak English. Our guide, Marcos Ramirez, a young guy in his twenties, who has recently left mining in order to further his education, introduces himself and explains that he will address us in Spanish and then translate into English as we proceed on the tour.

We take off for Rancagua, a smaller city 76 Kilometers from Santiago, located at the base of the Andes. The trip to the mine will be approximately another hour as we traverse the very steep mountain passes with multiple switch-backs – much like the trip from south Reno up to Virginia City, but about twice as long.

Prior to 1911, it was a seven day trip by donkey from Rancagua to Sewell. In 1911, Braden Co. built a train from the valley to the mine and reduced the length of the trip to five hours. Luckily, Roscoe Wilkes was hired in 1914 and would have taken the train to Sewell. His ship would have docked in the major Chilean port, Valparaiso, and he probably travelled by train or bus to Santiago—a bus from Santiago to Rancagua and then taken the Braden train from Rancagua to Sewell. It more than likely would have been a two day trip, at least.

As we begin the incline up the mountains, the air is clearing, but the temperature is dropping. I'm a little jet-lagged, but giddy with expectation. The mountain formations are becoming steeper and taller—turning into veritable fifty-story, rocky sky-scrapers. I'm in the middle of these formations created by ancient glaciers, and I'm blown away.

We reach Sewell – I had seen photos on the internet which were slightly photo-shopped, but the reality— more gritty – is better, because it's real, and I'm living it.

Words are failing me. This place is really unique. There are probably about seven three-and-four story buildings remaining – tall, skinny buildings gathered together like siblings nestled into the skirts and slacks of their look-a-like parents, the Andes. They are well-dressed children, each sporting a different pastel color – one blue, one green, one pink.

All of the buildings perched on a severe incline are connected by an interlinking set of cement walkways and series of stair-steps which give the town its nickname, "Cuidad de las Escaleras," (City of Staircases.)

Marcos guides us first to the three storey social club, a very well preserved turn of the century building – massive wooden staircase and lots of wood trim. This building was for the American management, their friends and dignitaries. The social classes were well defined, so I doubt that Grandpa ever set foot in this elite building. However, the buildings for families and for single men were really state of the art for the early 1900's.

Mr. Braden had even built a four lane bowling alley in 1917, which remains intact and is positively adorable. Grandpa left in 1915; however, if he had seen that bowling alley, he might have stayed!

This company town thrived until the 1960's with a population reaching 15,000, including workers and families. However, President Montalva instituted a transfer of the population down to Rancagua in the valley due to the prevailing winds, which were carrying toxic sulfur-hydroxide fumes from the Caletones smelter. Now all of the miners live in Rancagua and ride buses to the mine.

3:00 P.M.—we've toured all of the buildings, even the ones which were not safe (It's Chile), and looked across the narrow ravine to the portals—the entrances to the working mine. It's windy, very chilly and time to leave Sewell. I have mixed emotions. I'm cold and hungry and want to leave, but I'm also sad— I don't want to leave Grandpa. I've convinced myself while walking in his footsteps that he is there with me.

As the bus is winding its way down the sides of the steep mountains, we pass at least thirty, older-looking buses filled with Chilean miners on their way to work. It's nearing 4:00 p.m., and it's time for the night shift to relieve the day shift.

The tour ends at a large Hacienda in the valley, which has been converted into a small event center to host weddings, receptions and tours. We are treated to a hearty roast beef and potato dinner.

Now, back to my original questions – have I figured out what this grandpa was all about? Would I have liked him? Would he have liked me? Are we more connected now that I have travelled in his footsteps to Sewell, Chile? I think the only way to determine the answers to these questions is to write a letter to grandpa and see what comes out!

Dear Grandpa,

You are a very intriguing guy. I have followed every inch of your life's journey except for a few periods when you dropped off the grid.

I have pondered for months what you were really like as a man. Were you a man of many words like your son, or fewer words like your daughter? Were you a story-teller like both of your children? Were you ambitious and a hard-worker? Did you like to be with people or be by yourself? Did you have a sense of humor? I think I've been able to answer some of these questions by deduction.

You must have liked stories, as this runs through both of your children. I also think you must have been somewhat extroverted, because both of your children were, and because you seemed to have made friends during your travels evidenced by photos, such as the picture of unidentified North Americans – male and female – entitled "Friends in Peru;" and evidenced by your repeated inquiry in the letter from Tybo, Nevada, asking grandma to write back with all the news about folks in Pioche; and, lastly, evidenced by your seeming willingness to live for months at a time in dormitories with other miners.

Grandpa, you were thrown off the family farm as a teenager, and left to make your own way in a big world. You had the physical and psychic energy to push forward, trying out different careers and ways of living while searching for a better life. You were a Wyoming cowboy, you ran a pool hall, you were a teamster, you were a barber, and you had a major mining career in silver and copper, working your way up to a Superintendent.

The vagaries of the mining industry, the loss of your hearing, and perhaps the lack of interest in playing the long game, took you down the backside of life's roller coaster. But, grandpa, that's not all bad— life is a journey that is played out on uneven ground. You were a man of the exciting times in which you lived. No doubt I would have liked you; and you would have liked me, because I would have made sure that you did!

With love and respect for a life well-lived,
Karen Wilkes, your very proud granddaughter

P.S. Thanks for leaving me a rich mining heritage. And, by the way, Aunt Kathryn gave me Grandma's gold wedding band and yours, as well; and my husband and I have proudly worn them for 22 years. We actually celebrated our 22nd wedding anniversary in South America and raised a toast to you!

Roscoe Wilkes

Roscoe and Estella Maud
Kathryn and Roscoe Jr.

PARIS

by
Karen Wilkes

(Written for the funeral of Roscoe Wilkes, Jr. in March of 2013, at Thompson's Opera House in Pioche, Nv.}

They say this place is too remote and inaccessible;
Too high in elevation; the winter's too long.

But, this is my Paris, says he.

Her hills are scarred and battered;
She lost all her jewels to con artists and thieves.
She's a washed up old floozy, who nobody needs.

Au contraire, she's a beauty like no other;
For she is my Paris, says he.

But, there are no salons, Eiffel Tower or vineyards;
No river runs through it, says we.

Take off your glasses man, and look hither with your heart;
You'll see Paris, like me.

But, now you're gone, we cry angrily!
You're gone!

Oh no; I'm not gone; you're wrong.
My ashes are here;
And, I am here;
For this is my Paris, you see.

PAUL T. BARNES, JR.

Nevada Miner

Life On the "A" List

Paul T. Barnes Jr. posts on *Facebook*, June 25, 2016; 2:32 p.m.:

"Have Yacht Rock on Sirius playing Pablo Cruise and all of a sudden I'm 30 again standing behind the wheel of "Samarang" heading out of Newport Harbor for Catalina. Sails going up... Ahhhh!"

At the young age of 30, Paul Barnes, semi-retired, had become the captain of a 62-ft. schooner docked in the Newport Beach harbor. He was living an enviable life in the fast lane of southern California – a fantasy life for most of us.

I first met Paul Barnes at my wedding in October of 1994. As we divided up the "to do" planning list, Darryl said, *"I'll take care of the music for the reception – I know a great group of guys in Boulder City who have put together a pick-up band, and several of these guys have played in famous bands."*
"H*mmmm*," I said. "*What could possibly go wrong?"*

James Quill Smith was the leader of the band. Smith was one of the original members of *"Three Dog Night"* and was the band member who was electrocuted in the 60's—not fatally—on stage in Spain when the cord to his guitar shorted out. We always wondered about James, *"was it the electrocution or the drugs that did the most damage?"* Another member of this band was Darryl's friend, Paul Barnes, Jr.

Greatly inspired by Neil Young, Paul Barnes had taught himself to play the guitar when he was 17. Hanging around southern California, he had made the acquaintance of the music producer, Norm Sancho, and of Jack Tempchin, who wrote for the Eagles. Through these connections, Paul played with some of the best musicians in L.A., honing his guitar abilities and still practicing two hours most days.

We would run into Paul every so often after the wedding. In 2010, Paul married the artist and musician, Nancy Good. My husband had coincidentally opened an art gallery in downtown Las Vegas, and Nancy displayed many of her fine pieces there for several years. Thus, our relationship with Paul was renewed, and I discovered that he had a very long history in mining in California and Nevada, which led to our collaboration on this story.

In the early 80's, Paul had the best of everything – a prestigious position as the captain of a yacht – a position that came with full entree to gorgeous, lanky, golden-tanned women, and the best alcohol and drugs that the 80's had to offer (of which he partook to his detriment). He held a strong position in stock and commodity markets and one-third ownership in a small oil company. What's more, he was hanging out with famous southern California musicians, writers, and producers – Paul was living life on the "A" list.

However, the truth of the matter was that Paul's life looked better on paper. Since his early teens, Paul had made a point of always taking the path less traveled, which brought him in close contact with the most interesting people. In fact, Paul had learned his sailing craft from a group of swarthy, sea-faring, southern California cannabis smugglers who were, indeed, the best sailors on the high seas of the Pacific coast. Once you had learned to sail under their conditions, there would be no other conditions more challenging in the career of a sea captain.

By age 16, Paul had come to the conclusion that he wanted nothing to do with either of his parents, so at age 17 he bought a car, dropped out of school, and left home. If his parents wanted to live a life of dysfunction, he would beat them at their own game and on his own turf and terms. He lived in a trailer in San Bernardino, owned by his dad, and went to work at the San Bernardino Rocket gas station. He soon fell madly in love, fathered his precious daughter, Jennifer, and got married, in that order. It was 1972—Paul was an 18 year old young man with a wife, a child, no education and a job at the Rocket gas station. He had also adopted habits of excessive alcohol and drug usage, and the bottom was nowhere in sight.

Eventually Paul entered the construction industry, and became a custom cabinet maker in Orange County, California. He stayed married to his childhood bride until he was 26, got a GED and took some college classes. Around this time he also signed up for a standardized aptitude test, which was very revealing. The test administrator told Paul that he could do anything at all in the world that he wished to do. The test showed that Paul had no limiting factors in any field— none—nada! That means that our Paul had the aptitude to be an astronaut; C.E.O. of a Fortune 500 Company; or a poet laureate.

Meet the Parents

We must backtrack now, because it is impossible to know Paul T. Barnes Jr., without understanding Paul T. Barnes Sr. And you will have no luck at all understanding this story until you know how the path of Paul Barnes Sr. intersects with Clyde Keegel, a graduate of the University of Nevada, Mackay School of mines.

Paul T. Barnes Sr. was born Oct. 29, 1903, in Ann Arbor, Michigan. He majored in engineering in college but did not graduate; however, he was grand-fathered in due to his extensive work experience. He attended the University of Nevada at Reno in 1923-1924, and the University of California at Berkley, 1925-1926. Did you ever wonder who invented the first aluminum shower door? Well, the answer to this *"Jeopardy"* question is: Paul T. Barnes Sr. and his partner, Homer Allen, invented the aluminum shower door in 1927.

He had become a pilot in the late 1920's surviving a plane crash in his private plane at the Boulder City airport, where he met Howard Hughes. But, more significantly, he met his second wife, also a pilot, who became the mother of his first child, Paula. The marriage did not last, and Paula lived with her mother after the divorce.

In 1943, Paul Sr. came to Nevada to work at Basic Magnesium in Henderson where he developed lasting relationships with several co-workers, primarily with Clyde Keegel. They both joined the Manhattan project and relocated to China Lake Naval Ordinance Test Station in the Mojave Desert. Clyde invented the measuring devices for the first nuclear blast, while Paul Sr. worked on other projects which are still classified and unknown to the public.

Clyde was bothered by the social and environmental aspects of the Manhattan project and tried to call foul, but his warnings were not heeded, and he ultimately left the project. His reservations were understandable, as the magnitude of these blasts was 1000-fold greater than the power of the Atom bomb. Paul Sr., however, liked the challenge of the work and stayed on, eventually moving to Eniwetok in the Marshall Islands as project engineer and remained there through all of the nuclear tests at that location.

At the end of the Eniwetok experiment, Paul Sr. returned to China Lake as a design engineer on rocket fuel systems where he obtained multiple patents for the Navy and was the recipient of two national design awards. During this time, Paul Sr. became a mentor to Marshall Kriesel who built his own rocket. Paul was influential in talking the Navy into launching the rocket. This event was covered by *Life* Magazine issue of Sept. 15, 1961, which includes a picture of Paul Sr. Kriesel told Paul Jr. in 2014 that his father had, in fact, designed the fuel control system for the lunar lander before they pulled the plug on the project. Kriesel graciously sent Paul the design file which is now unclassified.

All of this was accomplished without a formal engineering degree or knowledge of computers. Everything chronicled above was done with a slide rule and drawn by hand – *"He was just a genius with a slide rule,"* says son, Paul, Jr.

Paul Sr. met Eunice Ross at China Lake, and they were married in 1952. The next year, on Nov. 20, 1953, Eunice gave birth to Paul T. Barnes Jr. Paul Sr. was 50 years old when he became a father for the second time, and Eunice was 36.

Paul Sr. was a singularly talented engineer with gifts for design and problem solving which took him to the cutting edge of technology in the 1950's, and ultimately to hold a Department of Energy Q Clearance. He was also gifted with a work ethic honed by hardships during the Great Depression, which propelled him to tremendous success in his field.

Eunice was an intellectual equal to Paul Sr.—an incredibly gifted woman with talents which led her to teaching in two separate disciplines at the college level – Psychology and English. There was one very large problem. Although Paul Sr. and Eunice were both exceptionally multi-talented people in their individual careers, neither one of them had the needed skills to be a parent.

If there had been a screening system for who could be allowed to procreate, Paul Barnes Sr. and Eunice Ross would both have been rejected, as they both had problems with alcohol. But this is not how biology works in our universe. Paul Jr. drew the lucky card and was, indeed, delivered by the stork to the door of Paul T. and Eunice Barnes, China Lake, California.

With his parents fighting constantly, Paul Jr. was in full rebellion by age four or five and started running away at any opportunity. He was convinced by that early age that he did not belong to these two parents. Paul Sr. and Eunice divorced in 1963, when Paul was ten – no surprise there! Paul Sr., as accomplished as he was in his career, had no social skills and was terribly scarred from the depression era. He had become severely miserly as well as unreasonably mean–spirited. He was also unbelievably intolerant of his only son, Paul. Paul reports, *"He tried in every way he could to break me, but he never did."*

Paula, Paul Sr.'s daughter by his second wife, Kay, had come to live with the couple when she was 16—an ill-fated proposition—and Paula subsequently ran away. Paul Jr. never saw his half-sister again until locating her when he was 42. The two siblings, both of whom remarkably transcended their upbringing, remained in contact, but Paula was diagnosed with cancer in June 2016, and succumbed to the disease the following October.

After his parents divorced, Paul lived with his dad from age 10 to age 13, at which time he moved in with his mom. Eunice was an alcoholic, but was a very high functioning alcoholic – never missed work, and seemed o.k. most of the time. She had an opposite personality to that of her husband. Paul Jr. reports, *"If you open the Encyclopedia Britannica to 'Life of the party,' you would find a picture of my mother."* Living with mom meant people and parties all the time. This couple represented total opposite poles of the social spectrum – neither extreme being conducive to raising a wholesome child.

The cause of the extreme dysfunction in each of Paul's parents would take a team of psychologists to figure out. Why a man like Paul Sr., with all of the incredible success he had attained, would want to be so hard on his son, is beyond me. If I could meet with him in the afterlife, my one question would be, *"Mr. Barnes, with all of the strength, tenacity, and aptitudes that drove you to the greatest successes in our society, what made you think that you would have a son that you could easily control?"* I rest my case.

Salts & Demons

Now, how does Clyde Keegel fit into this story? While working at China Lake in the early 1950's, Paul Sr. started prospecting with his former colleague from Basic Magnesium and the Manhattan project, Clyde Keegel. Prospecting was a passion for Clyde, a chemical engineer, but a hobby for Paul Sr. By the time he was five years old, Paul Jr. was accompanying his dad and Clyde on their outings around Searle's lake, a California salt aquifer. Not particularly fond of prospecting at first, he became one of the team in due time. Since Paul Jr. had inherited his dad's aptitudes and tenacity, he knew more by age 12 about aquifer salts than most metallurgical engineers.

Clyde P. Keegel attended UCLA and graduated from University of Nevada Mackay School of Mines at Reno in 1938, with majors in mining and metallurgy. He was licensed in Nevada as a mining and metallurgical engineer and in California as a chemical engineer. He came from a southern Nevada mining family and had lived in the State most of his life. Keegel had been acting Vice President and manager of the Halliburton subsidiary in Honduras and had headed the Cuban subsidiary of Basic Refractories, a corporation which had developed large reserves of chromium ore.

Clyde introduced Paul Sr. to Frank Darrow in Trona, California, and Frank Balcar of Cleveland. Clyde, Paul Sr., and Balcar formed "Searles Lake Chemical Company" in 1954, with the help of attorney David Denny. The partnership purchased options from Darrow to ripen sodium and boron leases. After drilling the lake and proving it had high value, they brought in a large investor, Ray T. Miller, the former mayor of Cleveland. When a payment of $75,000 came due on the option in 1955, Searles Lake Chemical Co. could not perform. The partners had already spent $75,000 of their own money ripening the leases, so Miller made the payment, but demanded 51% of the stock in return.

At that point, Ray Miller hired a new attorney, his son, Richard Miller, and the Searles Lake Chemical Corp. began a legal walk-about lasting from 1955 until 1996, involving leases that were signed but not recorded by the attorney; deals struck and lawsuits filed without notification to all of the interested parties; the creation of a questionable trust; agreements to purchase Capital Stock not included in Royalty agreements; and assignments of royalties never known to the three original partners.

By 1996, the companies now involved in the mining of Searles Lake were Occidental Petroleum, Kerr-McGee, Leslie Salt, Arco, and North American Chemical Co. The original three partners did not have the resources to continue hiring lawyers who could compete with the legal maneuvering of the teams of lawyers funded by these large corporations, so they ended up with no rights to any leases and no royalties.

Searles Lake has been called the single richest mineral deposit in the world, containing 98 of the world's 100 most valuable minerals. The lake mainly produces sodium and boron products with estimated gross sales of approximately $400,000,000 per year; and these corporations can continue production at this rate for another 400 years.

Paul Sr. had spent most of his savings on this project and was thoroughly disgusted with "salts;" but Clyde Keegel, a "died in the wool" miner, was undaunted. In the 1950's he purchased potassium leases at Silver Peak in Clayton Valley, Nevada, about 25 miles outside of Goldfield, Nevada and 200 miles from Searles Lake.

Fast forward to 1979. Paul had been working as a cabinet maker for several years when he reunited with his father and joined him in the oil business in Pennsylvania and

Oklahoma. Paul Sr. had quit drinking, but Paul Jr. had not – now heavily into alcohol and cocaine as a cure for the alcohol abuse. Then, to make matters worse, the bottom fell out of the oil market, Paul Jr.'s strong positions in the silver market vanished, and Paul Sr.'s health was failing.

In 1982, Paul met the artist, Robin Temaiana, in Newport Beach and was, once again, in love. Robin gave birth to Paul's precious second daughter, Brooke Barnes. However, Paul was still partying in excess which never lends itself to a continuing relationship, and the couple separated.

By this time, life on the "A" list in L.A. was starting to wear very thin. Paul decided to make a sharp left turn, and in 1984 he totally quit all alcohol and drugs, which was 95 days before his father's death on January 1, 1985. He was told by a counselor that with the magnitude of his addictions, he should be admitted into an in-patient treatment facility for one to two years, or he most definitely would not be successful in sobriety. However, this counselor did not know Paul Barnes Jr. and his inherited genetic disposition. All of the good genes that Paul had inherited from both parents were called forth, and Paul led those genes into basic training, formed a regiment, and started his own personal war on drugs. He went to two or three AA meetings per day for over three years. Although he remained clean and sober, it took that long before Paul could go one full day without having major mental and emotional battles with his addiction. In the process of what amounted to guerilla warfare waged within, Paul, with the help of counselors and AA sponsors, worked through the family problems with his parents and came out the other side a changed man. Paul did, indeed, defy the odds and has been sober now for 32 years – an astonishing accomplishment.

The Making of a Miner

Paul Barnes Jr., now a mentally and physically strong, mature man, was ready to make his way in the world and wanted to make up for lost time. In 1987, he started thinking that with the knowledge he had gained from years of prospecting with his dad and Clyde, that he could, perhaps, make some extra money in mining. So, Paul called his dad's old buddy, Clyde Keegel, whom he had always admired, and inquired if they might do some prospecting together. Clyde, having known Paul Jr. since he was knee-high to a grasshopper, said, *"Yes, let's give that a try."* They started prospecting for gold in Goldfield, Nevada, drilling holes looking for deposits that had possibly been overlooked during the boom years there.

Paul was by then working as an exhibit builder in Costa Mesa, California, driving back and forth to Goldfield at every opportunity to pursue the prospecting. The two spent countless hours, days, weeks and months in the desert, tromping through snow in the winters, and enduring incredible heat in the summers. By the end of two years, they had bonded almost as father and son. Paul reminisces that,

"Socially, Clyde was the opposite of my father. He had a wonderful sense of humor, was a small man in stature, but tough as nails when he had to be and absolutely fearless. Along with my father and Frank Balcar, Clyde is one of the three most incredible men I have ever known. I have always thought of them as the three wise men."

This must have had an incredible healing effect on Paul, but as much fun as they were having together, the partnership had not come up with any new minerals to mine.

One day in early 1989, Clyde says to Paul, "*Let's take a ride over to Silver Peak?*" Since Clyde is the senior prospector and the one with credentials, Paul readily agrees. They arrived and took a look at the area which Foote Mineral Co. was mining for Lithium. Clyde, a very experienced mining and metallurgical engineer, makes an off-handed comment, "*Ya know, if a guy was smart he would file for potassium prospecting permits around here.*" Then Clyde just drove away and never said one other word about his comment or about Silver Peak – ever!

Somehow, Paul, intuitively, did not feel like he could press Clyde any further about the subject. However, he also intuitively felt that if this is what Clyde said, that he meant it; and that Paul, if he were in fact a smart guy, should do what Clyde recommended. And, we know by now that Paul is, indeed, a very smart guy, and a guy with no short amount of follow-through. I am quite convinced that Clyde also knew this about Paul. This could not have been a random act on the part of Clyde Keegel – he was passing a baton.

The BLM (Bureau of Land Management) was the provider of such permits, so Paul, not a guy to leave any stone unturned, quickly put together a small partnership of buddies and hastened to the nearest BLM office in Tonopah, Nevada. On May 31, 1989, Paul applied for a potassium prospecting permit on top of the property being mined for lithium by Foote Mineral Co.

Meet the new Paul T. Barnes, Jr. – the guy who has legally come head to head with Cypress Foote Corporation, aka. Chemetall Foote Corp, their parent company, Rockwood Holding Co, the BLM, and the Department of the Interior over leasing rights to minerals which appear in the marshy brines in Clayton Valley, better known as Silver Peak, just 55 miles east of the historic mining towns of Tonopah and Goldfield, Nevada.

Silver Peak is one of the oldest mining camps in Nevada, with its early bonanza occurring in 1865. It had its bonanzas and borrascas for 38 years accompanied with the building of several stamp mills and a small railroad, but became a near ghost town in 1917. The town burned in 1948 and had virtually been reclaimed by the Nevada desert when Foote Mineral Company began the extraction of lithium from the subterranean aquifer under the floor of Clayton Valley.

This area is high desert at an elevation of 4321 ft. There are several fairly high mountain ranges nearby, separated by really long expanses of hot, white, flat-as-a-spatula, deserts. The dry lake bed, from which the aquifers rise, is 17 miles long and 5 ½ miles wide. It is 100 miles from Death Valley, 55 miles east of Tonopah, 80 miles southeast of Hawthorne and 100 miles east of Bishop, California. In other words, when hanging out at Silver Peak, it's not easy to run out for a pack of cigarettes.

The current lithium mine consists of a few buildings, multiple really large ponds filled with very stale looking brine, and more ponds with snow white tailings, which remain after the brine has evaporated. There are miles of black PVC pipe connecting the various ponds, as the brine is moved through these pipes from one pond to another for evaporation purposes.

Trampin' in, pard? Oh, you better believe it! And now, we have us a real, honest to goodness Nevada mining story about a real honest to goodness Nevada miner, and you won't want to miss it.

On May 31, 1989, as previously stated, Paul T. Barnes, Jr., based on the advice of Clyde Keegel, applied for prospecting permits for potassium on patented lands at Silver Peak, Nevada. The permits were suspended on November 6th of that year by the BLM due to litigation between the mining leasee, Chemetall Foote Corp, and the lessor, which would be the U.S. Department of the Interior. The permits were cheap at 50 cents per acre, so Paul put the suspension notice aside and forgot about it. When the permits were suspended, all of the partners dropped out, and nothing happened until 2007.

Out of the blue, in 2007, Stephanie Porter, Land Law Examiner for the BLM in Nevada, called Paul and asked him if he had filed for a prospecting permit in 1989, and, if so, did he still want it? He said, *"yes,"* and she said she would get back to him. Three weeks later, Ms. Porter called and told him there were stockpiles of potassium on the property, tailings from the mining of the lithium, and asked if he wanted those as well? To which he also replied *"Yes."* Another three weeks went by and Ms. Porter called again, stating that Paul could not have the stockpiles, because there had been a settlement agreement between the litigating parties, but their office had not received a copy of it, and they would have to review it before they could reinstate Paul's permit.

Three more weeks passed, and, once again, Ms. Porter called and said there is a settlement agreement between Chemetall Foote and the U.S. Government, and, per the terms of the agreement, Paul could not mine for potassium until the lithium was mined out. Paul's permit was once again suspended. Subsequent to this communication, Paul was told that Ms. Porter had been transferred by the BLM to the Everglades, after which she subsequently left the BLM. We, of course, are not sure if the Barnes matter was the catalyst for the transfer.

This is the point where Paul starts to become suspicious – our miner is no fool, and he has been around salt minerals all his life while hanging out with his dad and Clyde Keegel – and he certainly knows a bad brine when he smells it!

What is Lithium, Anyway?

The next part of Paul's story is very detailed, and it helps to have a working understanding of the minerals that Paul was intending to mine—potassium and lithium. This is verbatim text from my interview with Paul about these minerals:

Q. *What is lithium?*
A. *Lithium is an alkali metal.*
Q. *What are its historical uses?*
A. *Historically used for greases, production of glass, antidepressant drugs and necessary for reaction in hydrogen bombs.*
Q. *What are its uses now?*
A. *All of the above, plus lithium batteries and illegal methamphetamine production.*
Q. *What does lithium look like   feel like- smell like?*
A. *White salt. No smell. Taste is salty; extremely bitter.*
Q. *Where does it usually appear geologically?*
A. *In brines and silicates associated with sodium, magnesium and potassium and in spodumene hardrock deposits.*
Q. *How do you get it out of the ground?*
A. *Brines are pumped out of the ground into ponds.*
Q. *Does it then need processing? If so, what is the usual processing method?*
A. *Sodium and magnesium salts are harvested in that order from ponds leaving concentrated potassium 95% and lithium 5% to be pumped into the chemical plant to extract lithium - with potassium left to be processed or stored.*
Q. *How much is it worth? How much volume do you need to extract to make how much money? i.e. price per ton?*

A. Lithium Carbonate price today is $20,000 per ton. Potassium Chloride $270 per ton. Minimum production would be about 100,000 tons per year for potassium alone to be profitable with lithium profit exceeding.

At the risk of providing too much detail about lithium, I think this mining story is not complete without at least two full paragraphs—maybe three—about how this mineral is mined!

Jerome A. Lukes, mining engineer, describes it this way in a letter to James L. Wadsworth, attorney for Leprechaun Mining and Chemical Co.

> "…brine from the wells is pumped into solar ponds where the brine is concentrated. The partially concentrated brine is then transferred to the lime treatment, where the addition of lime causes magnesium hydroxide to precipitate. Magnesium is removed in the ponds so that in the lithium recovery plan the sodium carbonate consumption is reduced.
>
> From the liming step, the nearly magnesium-free brine is transferred to another set of ponds where additional evaporation concentrates the lithium values to near lithium sulfate saturation. During this concentration step, potash crystallizes along with other salts to form a mixture of potassium chloride, potassium sodium sulfate, sodium chloride and calcium potassium sulfate. These salts build up in the ponds and periodically are removed and stored in a stockpile.
>
> The high lithium brine from the potash ponds is pumped to the lithium carbonate plant, where it is first treated to remove calcium and small amounts of magnesium. After this so-called cleanup step, the high lithium brine is treated with sodium carbonate. The carbonate from the sodium carbonate reacts with the lithium in the brine to crystallize lithium carbonate. The solid lithium carbonate is then removed, dried and stored."

And I conclude, If it was easy, everyone would be doing it!

Paul, in the meantime, had moved to Boulder City, Nevada, and had married again. He had entered the fast moving construction industry during the Las Vegas boom years—late 1990's and early 2000's—rising to a construction project manager for a hotel and casino building contractor.

Unfortunately, in 1991, his new wife, Janice, was diagnosed with a very aggressive Lupus condition, and the couple began a nine year battle for her life. Paul was not thinking about his suspended potassium permits at Silver Peak. In fact, he had completely forgotten about even filing them, when that unexpected phone call came from the BLM's Stephanie Porter.

It is also important to know at this point that lithium never appears by itself in brine (never, ever). It only appears in brines with other salts, such as sodium or potassium. The final brine going into the processing plant consists of a very specific percentage of 6% lithium and 94% potassium for optimum production of lithium carbonate. Any deviation from this ratio in either direction can cause the process to fail. So, anyone mining lithium anytime and anywhere ends up with a pile of potassium which is 9.4 times as large as the pile of lithium. Of course, the potassium is not worth anything near the value of the lithium but, be that as it may, you will still have a huge pile of potassium to reckon with. You can sell it at whatever the going value is; or you can stockpile it, hoping the value will go up so you can sell it later. But, the bottom line is that it will not evaporate, dissipate, or disappear – not ever.

As far as Paul knew at the time of filing his permit application, Foote Mineral Co. had no interest in potassium. Keegel had said, "*They are only mining lithium.*" It would be many years, long after Keegel was gone, before Paul discovered the real story. What Paul also did not know was that Keegel was teaching him where and how to find information that he would later need, by charging him with hours of research in the UNLV library on other mining projects and mining law. Paul would ultimately end up at the same library 20 years later, searching for the truth.

The Brine Thickens

Minerals are classified as "Leasable" or "Locatable." How a miner would stake a claim to prospect or drill in an area for a mineral is directed by State and Federal laws – with the Federal laws being further defined and regulated by the Department of Interior, and under them, the Bureau of Land Management. For a miner to follow the appropriate regulations, he or she would need to know if the particular mineral at hand was "leasable" or "locatable."

"Leasable" minerals are explored for and developed in accordance with the Mineral Leasing Act of 1920, other leasing acts, and the Bureau of Land Management regulations. Leasable minerals today include oil and gas, oil shale, geothermal resources, potash, sodium, native asphalt, solid and semi-solid bitumen, bituminous rock, phosphate, sulfur and coal. The 1920 Mineral Leasing Act further stipulates that **royalties** must be paid to the U.S. government when extracting these minerals. Most generally, if a second mineral is always found in a brine with the leasable mineral, the secondary mineral would also be leasable.

"Locatable" minerals are any minerals not leasable or salable, and are managed under the General Mining Law of 1872 and BLM regulations (43CFR 3700 and 3800). Typical locatable minerals are gold, silver, copper, gemstones, lead, zinc, barite, gypsum, certain varieties of high calcium limestone, and molybdenum.

In general, minerals that are solid and can be fairly recognizable one from another in an ore matrix are "locatable." Any liquid mineral that might appear in a liquid state with other minerals would be "leasable."

The 1872 Mining Law grants U.S. citizens the right to prospect, explore and develop these "locatable" minerals on public domain lands that have not been "withdrawn" from mineral entry by Congress or the Secretary of the Interior. Under this law, the miner must file a mining claim to proceed, but **royalties** are not due to the Government when extracting the minerals. The miners are to pay taxes when the minerals are sold, as in real estate, cattle ranching or any other business that sells a product, but they would not owe royalties.

These original mining laws were written shortly after the gold rush in California and in Nevada, and were highly influenced by the mining lobbyists of the day, who, in effect, were writing the laws and just submitting them to the legislators. The mining industry had just exploded with the recent discoveries of gold and silver, and the leaders of the industry had become extremely rich and powerful in very few years, running roughshod over a new and wobbly State government. The government was, however, by the 1920 Mineral Leasing Act, able to gain some ground in taxing the revenue of the new liquid minerals being mined.

As per the 1954 Mining Act, however, the "leasable" minerals, the salts, potassium, lithium, etc., needed a permit to even prospect, and those permits are issued "at the will" of the BLM. Therefore, the Government can now control who prospects for leasable minerals by the fact that they control who gets the permits. They can give permits and they can take them away, as Paul Barnes had learned when his potassium permits for Silver Peak were offered to be issued along with stock piles of potassium, and then three weeks later were suspended indefinitely due to the pending litigation.

In September of 2007, shortly after Paul was contacted by Stephanie Porter of the BLM about the stockpiled potassium, he drove to the mine at Silver Peak to take a look around. As soon as he drove onto the property, his truck became surrounded by multiple other trucks blocking his further entrance or exit. Eventually the Manager of Chemetall Foote, Joe Dunn, appeared and said, *"You're a big topic of conversation in these parts, and you can't be on this property."* Paul tried to diffuse the suspicious nature of the conversation and replied, *"Let's do something together."* Joe Dunn said he would pass the offer on to the boss and let Paul go. Paul judiciously decided to leave peacefully. Of course, the bosses did not call.

Upon further reflection, Paul came to the very naive conclusion that his possession of the potassium permits must give him some leverage, even if they were in suspension; and that he should try to negotiate with the mining companies to see if there might be the possibility of developing some type of a partnership. He called Ron France, the CFO of Foote Mineral Company (now Chemetall Foote Co.) and said again, *"Let's do something together."* Mr. France said he was open to the idea.

Paul also contacted the general manager of Great Salt Lake Minerals, (GSM), Ron Bryan. GSM was currently producing potassium sulfate out of the Great Salt Lake, and according to Mr. Bryan, *"We could always use more."* Mr. Bryan agreed to meet with Paul in Las Vegas and they conducted a short meeting at McCarran Airport, which concluded with the agreement to pursue it further. Paul then contacted Mr. France and was able to set up a three way meeting at the Great Salt Lake Mineral's headquarters in Overland Park, Kansas.

Prior to the meeting, Paul had serendipitously made a new friend in the processing side of this business, who told Paul not to be intimidated in the meeting with the Chemetall Foote representative, because none of them knew any more than Paul did about processing potassium, although they were beginning to educate themselves on the subject.

The meeting did take place, but nothing was decided. The next day an e-mail arrived from Great Salt Lake Minerals to Chemetall Foote asking, *"Where does the potassium come from?"* They wanted to determine this before they got further involved. Chemetall Foote replied, *"We don't know where the potassium comes from—that it just comes up in the brine from the acquifer."* This answer did not satisfy Great Salt Lake Minerals, and they backed out of any further negotiations. Then Chemetall Foote backed out, as well.

Paul's second attempt at making a deal was with Olin Corp., a manufacturer of potassium hydroxide. The outcome of this contact was that Olin and Chemetall engaged in private discussions excluding Paul.

Paul's next step was to approach Chemetall's parent company, Rockwood Holdings, Inc. He contacted their vice-president of investor relations on Feb. 19, 2009, to share with him ideas he had regarding lithium and potassium production in addition to the production of geothermal, which would be beneficial to all the stake holders. Paul had investigated the possibility of obtaining a government grant for expanding the Silver Peak operation, as it had great promise for clean energy through the use of the lithium for electric car batteries. The executives indicated that they were not interested. However, one month later they filed for this exact grant (application #SF424), and they were awarded the grant in the amount of approximately $37,000,000 to expand lithium production and drill for geothermal resources at Silver Peak.

Paul did not receive a thank you note, a phone call or a gift basket for his part in making the Rockwood executives aware of this grant opportunity. However, this back-fired in part, as Rockwood was not able to drill for geothermal within the boundary of Paul's application areas, and, therefore, was outside the preferred target zone for geothermal. They came up empty handed.

Paul, now totally demoralized after his multiple attempts to work with these corporations, could not understand why they were so reticent. What really did they have to lose? Paul's permits could only enhance the operation for all of them, but they had backed out of any further negotiations, which was a tipping point for Paul. He finally came to the conclusion that he should pursue investors on his own and form a new company in order to mine the potassium himself. He put the invitation out to investors and quickly attracted attention.

A new consortium of investors was formed who began their due diligence process starting with the investigation of Paul and also the Silver Peak mine. They hired Holmes, Roberts and Owens in Denver for $30K to investigate Paul, and they ordered an engineering report from Agapito Associates, a respected Denver engineering company, to investigate the minerals available to be mined at Silver Peak. Agapito determined that there were 30 million tons of sodium missing from Chemetall's inventory, as well as an additional 15 million tons of potassium. With the amount of lithium being sold, there had to be "x" amounts of sodium and potassium coming out of the brine, as well. Where was it? The stock piles did not reflect the mathematically correct amount of tailings.

Leprechaun Mining and Mineral Co.

The salt marshes in Clayton Valley, central Nevada, originally attracted attention during World War II, during an effort by the Government to locate strategic minerals for use in manufacturing munitions. The original leases at Silver Peak were owned by American Potash, who was mining for potassium. They discontinued their operation at Silver Peak after the war and allowed their leases to expire. Clyde Keegel, always with his nose to the ground, as any good mining engineer should, picked up the defunct leases of American Potash.

On Sept. 16, 1954, he formed a corporation with several of his friends from southern Nevada, chartered as Leprechaun Mining and Chemical, Inc. Keegel was President; Roger L. Du Charme, Vice President and Secretary; Donn E. Ronnow Vice President, and Treasurer; and Robert E. Campbell, Vice President of Exploration. Also, Robert Zuber and Charles E. Ronnow were on the Board of Directors.

Clyde had met Robert Campbell while both were working in Cuba. Donn and Charles Ronnow were brothers, born and raised in Lincoln County, an area prolific in mining up until the early 1950's who both had relocated to southern Nevada – Donn became a contractor for the Atomic Energy Commission and Charles had gone into trucking and transport.

Once Clyde had proven the lithium and potassium at Silver Peak, Leprechaun Mining and Mineral Co. attracted the interest of Foote Mineral Company, who also had lithium mines in North Carolina and Atacama de Salar, Chile.

Leprechaun was able to sell their interest to Foote Mineral Co. in 1964, with the provision that Foote Mineral Co. would pay royalties on production of lithium and potassium to Leprechaun.

Leprechaun had never intended to mine Silver Peak. They had purchased the original leases for an investment, intending to sell or to sub-lease to a second company who would handle the actual mining operation, which is done quite frequently in the mining industry. They believed, of course, and, they were initially told, that both minerals would be mined by Foote Mineral Co. Foote mined the brines which contained sodium, potassium, magnesium as well as lithium, but they chose to sell only lithium, due to its value, and commenced stockpiling the other minerals. They did not want to pay royalties to the government or to Leprechaun on the other lesser valued minerals. It did not make business sense to them at the time to do so, or, so they said.

Paul knew nothing at all about any of this – absolutely nothing, because Clyde Keegel never brought up the subject of Leprechaun Mining Co. or anything at all related. Clyde passed away in 1998. In 2009, however, Paul found out accidentally that the last CEO of Leprechaun Mining, Donn Ronnow, had died, and that all of the Leprechaun Mining Co. records were donated by Ronnow's daughter to "special collections" at the UNLV library.

Paul drove immediately to the University, (he knew it well from his previous years of research driven by Clyde Keegel), where he was presented with 13 large boxes filled with the history of Leprechaun Mining. These boxes proved to be a treasure trove of information, indicating, in Paul's view, that Foote Mineral Company had possibly engaged in years of legal manipulation geared toward avoiding paying royalties to the Federal Government, and that the BLM, the Department of Interior, and that the Department of Justice had allowed this to happen—probably not on purpose—but by lack of attention to red flags.

The Leprechaun Mining and Chemical Inc. back-story goes as follows:

Clyde Keegel and his partners, after selling Leprechaun Mining Co. to Chemetall Foote in 1964, had not gotten along well with them, and the business partnership ended up in litigation with an eventual settlement. For some reason, prior to the sale to Foote Mineral Co., Clyde Keegel started pursuing Congressman Baring and the Nevada Senators at the time, Alan Bible and Howard Cannon, to introduce a bill into Congress to specifically define lithium as a leasable mineral. Why he was so adamant about this, we don't know, as lithium had always been considered leasable. But Clyde was, in fact, hell bent on getting the statutes on lithium clarified.

What did he know, and when did he know it? Did Clyde have some evidence that Chemetall Foote was intending to change the status of lithium? There just is not any other explanation as to why Clyde would go to all the effort that was needed to work with his Congressmen on this issue. Anyway, all three of the Congressmen were in agreement with him that this clarification of the law should be made, but they were unsuccessful. The Dept. of Interior was firm that the current statute of 1920 clearly implied that lithium was leasable and this would never change – there was no reason for a more detailed definition. This determination by the Department of Interior was made March 29, 1962.

In 1974, the BLM told Foote Mineral Co. that they needed to pay royalties on the potassium they were producing and stockpiling. The BLM also wanted to increase the percentage of royalties they were paying on lithium as well. They were pushing for a 50% increase. Corporations exist solely to make money – they have no other purpose. Therefore, a 50% increase in royalties would have a considerable effect on the bottom line – what to do? Foote's attorneys came up with a plan that if they could get the Government to change the definition of lithium to "locatable" as gold and silver, there would be no royalties owed what-so-ever. Problem solved!

Paul is not sure if they ever really thought they would be successful, as it was a long shot; but, unbelievably, they did. Foote Mineral Co. appealed to the Interior Board of Land Appeals (IBLA) with the argument that lithium should be locatable, because there is no potassium associated with it at Silver Peak of any value—therefore, in this instance, the lithium stands alone. The IBLA denied their request.

Foote Mineral Co. then appealed to the United States Court of Claims. Their sitting judge went back to the IBLA and asked them if they ever checked the property to determine if potassium was there? The IBLA says they did not take this step. The "Court of Claims" then determined July 1, 1981, that, because they (both BLM and IBLA) neglected to investigate, it has to be inferred that they agreed with Foote Minerals that there was "no potassium." So in this case, it means that lithium stands alone at Silver Peak, and is, therefore, locatable....Victory for Foote Minerals!

After the Department of Interior decided not to pursue this further, Foote filed to get a refund for the $600,000 in past royalties paid, and the Dept. of the Interior gave them the refund—second victory for Foote Minerals! Foote then paid only $37,000 for their new patents on the now "locatable" lithium ground, and they are off and running – third victory for Foote Minerals! (Except for the fact that the Land Patent issued November 25th, 1988, held the stipulation that all leasable minerals, meaning potassium and sodium, were reserved to the United States government and their permitees, lessees, or licensees.) And, Paul Barnes was a permitee, with a suspended permit.

But wait! Paul Barnes Jr. then comes along, and, without really knowing what he is doing, starts dredging up old records from the Leprechaun Mining Co. files at UNLV, shedding light on prior manipulations by Foote Mineral Co. Letters between Keegel and Foote's lawyers show that Keegel was getting bothersome to them, and Keegel is very blatantly told in writing by Foote's lead attorney and strategist, Mr. Randy L. Parcel (later to become a trustee on the Rocky Mountain Mineral Law Foundation 1993-94) that if Clyde starts revealing any negotiations, he will be dealt with very harshly—thus, a clear reason that Keegel does not reveal any details to Paul Jr.

However, it appears that by encouraging a third party, Paul Jr., to obtain the locatable permits for potassium, Clyde Keegel had, in fact, procured an "ace in the hole" for future use. To be safe, he did not breathe one word to Paul about Leprechaun Mining Co. and its dealings with Foote, which has now become Chemetall Foote. The less Paul knew, the better off they both would be in future negotiations – especially Clyde, since he was the one who was being threatened into silence.

Clyde was a great family man. He was married to Rose Keegel, half owner of the world famous *"Musso and Frank Grill"* on Hollywood Blvd., which she inherited from her father. She and Clyde had two beautiful daughters. Paul reports,

> *"It must have taken everything that Clyde had to hold back from exposing Foote after they threatened him, and he did it for the good of his family – not because he was afraid."*

Clyde Passes the Baton to Paul Jr.

Paul did not know much about Leprechaun Mining Co., other than the fact that they were the predecessor to Chemetall Foote at Silver Peak. He did not know that Leprechaun and Chemetall Foote had been in litigation over Silver Peak and had arrived at a settlement agreement in 1991. Clyde had left Paul operating totally in the dark, and Clyde knew it. Clyde did not want to take any further chances with the legal team representing Chemetall Foote and knew he had to stop biting their ankles. However, was it fair to encourage Paul to take action on the potassium leases without knowing all of these back stories with their raveled edges?

Fair or not, Clyde wasn't above making some mischief with a corporation, and he knew that the young Paul Barnes was just the guy to throw the bone to. He knew that once Paul picked it up, he would never let it go, as long as he felt he was in the right, and Clyde had given Paul the tools needed to follow the law.

The agreement between the government and Foote Mineral Co. was arrived at in 1991. Lithium was now locatable, but the government reserved the rights to all other leasable minerals, i.e., sodium, potassium and magnesium, and stipulated that these must be stockpiled by Foote on behalf of the government, and they must file annual reports documenting the size of the stockpiles and submit to regular inspections of the stockpiles and the contents of the brines. It's possible that Foote Mineral Co. had been stockpiling potassium in the underground empty ponds since the 1970's. Now, due to the new agreement in 1991, they could stockpile the potassium above ground and not pay royalties. Victory for Foote Mineral Co.!

Leprechaun and Foote argued over their agreement, and Leprechaun ended up filing a suit against Foote. The Leprechaun partners were getting older and they eventually determined that it was in their best interest to settle out of court, and they agreed to settle with Foote for a sum of $1,075,000 to be paid over a number of years. Leprechaun would still be due healthy royalties on any potassium mined and beneficiated by Foote outside of the Patented Lands. At the time of this settlement, for evaluation purposes, the potassium stock pile was documented at 2.6 million tons.

Back-tracking further, August 21, 1990, in a letter from Richard D. Mills, Senior Vice President and General Manager of Cyprus Foote Mineral (one of the interim names of Foote Mineral Co), he states,

> *"At our last meeting, I also indicated that Cyprus Foote has begun supplementing lithium values from the wellfield with lithium-containing salts from the Great Salt Lake. We are making the addition at a point just prior to liming. Based on past experience, we expect to recover 97.34% of this material in the plant. We are keeping detailed records of the quantities and quality of the material added to maintain a material balance in the strong brine complex in order to properly account for production of lithium carbonate from all sources.*
> *"We anticipate that Silver Peak will produce approximately 1,000,000 pounds of lithium carbonate from Great Salt Lake salts in 1991 and in excess of 2,000,000 pounds during subsequent years. Since this lithium carbonate derives from lithium-containing salts not originating in the Clayton Valley, we do not anticipate paying Leprechaun a royalty on the lithium carbonate produced from these salts...."*

Furthermore, on November 1, 1990, in another letter from the Vice President of Production of Cyprus Foote Mineral Company, P. J. Seaman,

> "It is our firm belief that the addition of the salts from the Great Salt Lake into our pond system is not detrimental to the Silver Peak operation. As far as obtaining samples, you are welcome to visit Silver Peak and take samples as requested in your letter. As for sampling the Great Salt Lake source, we will request that you be given access to the appropriate materials. We would like to have a representative present. If we cannot obtain permission on your behalf however, you are also welcome to sample the trucks as they unload at Silver Peak."

Whaaat!!!

Cyprus Foote is in the middle of a lawsuit with the United States concerning lithium deemed locatable by the prior lawsuit and the current disposition of leasable minerals from the same brines, and Cyprus is bringing in salts from the Great Salt Lake by the truckload and putting them into the pond system?

Where are they coming from? Cyprus wouldn't be buying salts to produce lithium would they? How could bringing salts in by truck 450 miles be profitable? Were they trading salts? What were they trading? There were many questions to be answered.

There is a memo in the Leprechaun files dated December 12, 1991, from Don Hendricks of Leprechaun to Donn Ronnow, the President, saying "that on review of documents in the litigation with Foote, there is evidence of Foote selling or trading salts prior to the 1991 settlement with the Government, in a manner possibly to avoid paying royalties. There is also a memo in the Leprechaun files from Don Ronnow to their then attorney, Ralph Denton of Las

Vegas, dated January 14, 1992, mentioning that Foote has been producing lithium from Magnesium Corporation's waste. This, of course, is speculation on the part of the Leprechaun partners."

Permits and Potassium Go Missing

In the meantime, Paul Jr. was never advised by the BLM, or by Clyde Keegel, of the 1991 settlement between Leprechaun Mining Co. and Foote Mineral Corp. He was totally left out of the loop, which he should not have been, as he held the potassium permit filed May 31, 1989, which was suspended entirely based on this very litigation. But, per this agreement of 1991, the U.S. Government now maintained rights to the potassium should there be any. Whose rights should be honored – Paul Barnes Jr., who holds a permit application for the potassium, or the U.S. Government which has made an end run around Mr. Barne's legal rights and has entered into an agreement with a corporation, allowing Foote to potentially retain the rights to the potassium?

Later the BLM contended that Paul's permits were misplaced, and they did not know about them until 2007 when Stephanie Porter, the Land Law Examiner, discovered them.

When Paul was contacted by Ms. Porter in 2007 regarding the missing application, he went to work to see if he could activate the permits. As he became more cognizant of the tangled web that had been woven, Paul began his attempts to work with Chemetall Foote Minerals and their parent company, Rockwood Holdings, to organize a joint venture, as he still saw this as his best bet. Paul was willing to put any past mistakes on the part of the BLM and/or Chemetall Foote behind him, and try to put together a workable deal which would rightfully include him as the bearer of the potassium permit. He wanted to move forward, not backward, if at all possible. But the parties start to shift their rationale as to why a joint venture would not work. As Paul analyzed these differing stories that were shifting to the right and then again to the left, his suspicions start to rise – "*What's up?*" Two and two are adding up to five.

When Paul's investors hired Agapito Associates, Inc., a noted mining engineering firm from Denver to evaluate the current sodium and potassium resources at Silver Peak, they discovered a huge shortfall of sodium and potassium – millions of tons unaccounted for. Silver Peak is very remote—224 miles from Reno and 213 miles from Las Vegas. There had been very few inspections by the BLM, and, perhaps, those that had been done might not have been done thoroughly.

Jerome Lukes, an engineer, had been hired by Leprechaun Mining Co. when they were establishing values of the mine during negotiations for the settlement with Foote. Lukes concluded in 1988, that the inventory of potassium was 875,000 tons, which was 76.9 percent of what was projected, resulting in a shortfall of 263,627 tons. This suggests that salts might have been disappearing prior to the Foote settlement with the Government in 1991.

In the year 2000, Galo Silva of the BLM documented 20 million tons of salts. In 2009, Agapito estimated between 4.7 and 6.5 million tons of potassium chloride had been produced up to that date. The BLM currently states there are approximately 5.5 million tons. It would appear that Galo Silva's estimates possibly were a glaring mistake that no one caught.

There are also two versions of a BLM memo that was discovered – one with two supervisors signing the memo and one with only one supervisor's signature. In this memo, dated May 2, 2002, Melissa Jennings, a supervisor for Chemetall Foote Minerals, inquires to the BLM about the possibility of Foote acquiring potassium leases without having to bid for them, an attempt that was repeated on November 5, 2008.

Foote argued to the Federal Court of Claims that lithium should not be leasable, because there was no potassium of value at Silver Peak—then, after winning their argument and filing mining claims, they argued that the potassium was a non-leasable byproduct of their mining operation. This was vehemently denied by Tom Leshendock, BLM Nevada Deputy State Director for Mineral Resources, which probably led to the reservation of leasable minerals paragraph in the Land Patent that was ultimately issued to Chemetall Foote.

Chemetall Foote Corp. can't have it both ways— or can they? They seem to have been very successful with every appeal to the BLM, the IBLA (Department of Interior Board of Land Appeals), and the Federal Grants Dept.

In May of 2009, Paul filed prospecting permit applications on all of the lithium claims at Silver Peak. Once again he decided to drive to Silver Peak to take a look around; and, as soon as he got close to the ponds, he discovered hundreds of super sacks (2,000 lb. bags) imprinted "Sociedad Chilena del Litio," a Chilean corporation owned by Chemetall Foote. These sacks contain the same lithium that is mined at Silver Peak. Why would a lithium mine import lithium from their other lithium mine in Chile?

Paul discovered that Chemtall Foote had been importing lithium salts for several years from the mine they own in Chile – Salar de Atacama. Between 2007 and 2009, 19 shipments averaging 110 to 250 tons per shipment were delivered to Silver Peak. The Nevada Department of Taxation shows the 2005 production at Silver Peak at $94,866, which is a figure so low that you ordinarily would close down the mine. In 2006, the production jumped to $3,173,652 and kept jumping every year hence.

Importing lithium to a known lithium mine and paying taxes on the production does not make sense. No corporation would do this. Could it be that Silver Peak is running out of lithium? Or, could it be that if you import lithium that you already own, but just pay taxes on it, you might be able to continue removing potassium without detection? And, if the potassium produced an income that was greater than the importation and taxation expenses of the lithium, and if you did not have to pay any royalties to the State of Nevada, perhaps you could make a profit? We can only speculate.

In December of 2009, Paul was once again nosing around in the Silver Peak area—why not—and stopped for coffee at the "Dusty Fenders Grill and Fill" now known as the "*Dinky Diner*", a café in Goldfield. Several local guys were holding up the counter. Paul nodded his head to the group, and they nodded back.

> One local speaks directly to Paul, "*So, are you with Chemetall Foote?*"
>
> Paul says a polite, "N*o*."
>
> The local, as he is slowly sizing Paul up, then says, "*So, ya with the EPA?*"
>
> Paul politely says, "N*o.*"
>
> The local, pausing with concern, rises from his chair, hitches up his work pants, and says, "*Well, then you must be the other guy. Are you here to hurt us or to help us?*"
>
> Paul replies, "*I'm here to help – I'm here to create some jobs.*"
>
> Local says, "*Stay right here – I need to go get something.*"

The local returns with a business card, and proceeds to tell Paul that Chemetall Foote has been launching solid lithium ingots into Silver Peak ponds with clay pigeon launchers. Hmmmm – Why?

Is this further evidence that they have run out of lithium at Silver Peak? At the very least they must add huge quantities of potassium to keep the ratio of potassium to lithium correct to process lithium. If so, why work so hard to keep this mine open? Chemetall Foote has other very large mining operations in North Carolina and in Chile. What is their motivation?

Paul Jr., being the tenacious over-achiever that he is, ended up, after trying to work with these corporations and determining in his own mind that they are possibly too corrupt to work with, contacted the Department of the Interior, making all of his suspicions known to them. The Department of the Interior decided to file an action against Chemetall Foote for conspiring to avoid paying Government-mandated royalties, and they use the "*Violations of Federal False Claims Act*" which requires a "whistle blower." Guess who? Paul Barnes Jr. is now the numero uno witness for the Department of Interior.

On April 29, 2011, U.S. Attorney Daniel G. Bogden rendered his decision for the defendant on the above whistle blower complaint against Chemetall Foote, via the whistle-blower, Paul T. Barnes, Jr., with a summary of the rationale as follows:

They sent an engineer hired by the government to Silver Peak to evaluate the size of the stockpiles of salts. They took photos of the piles today and compared them with the photos in the file from Galo Silva's BLM inspection of 2000. They determined that his documentation of the size of the stockpiles in 2000 was incorrect, causing the appearance of discrepancies afterwards. There is no mention in the Judges' decision of the fact that Agapito Assoc. from Denver, when doing due diligence for Paul's investors in 2009 came up with a 400,000 ton shortfall; or that Jerome Lukes, the engineer hired by Leprechaun in 1992, found a 263,627 shortfall – long before the BLM inspection in 2000.

They also sent out subpoenas to Great Salt Lake Minerals Corp. regarding possible purchases of Potassium from Silver Peak. Great Salt Lake Minerals replied that they have no records of any purchases of potassium from Silver Peak. However, there is no mention in the decision of whether they inquired about trade agreements.

U.S. attorney Bogden's investigators also concluded that, if Chemetall Foote was selling or trading large amounts of potassium, it would have to be trucked out, since there is no rail line in the area, and the increase in trucking from Silver Peak would have been noticed by the locals, and there is no evidence of increased trucking. They came up with a conclusion that it would take 80 trucks per day for 10 years to move the amount of potassium alleged missing.

These conclusions by the U.S. attorney's office are understandable and worthy of analysis; however, would not the conclusions have carried more weight if they had taken the investigation just a little further.

I do feel that they should have procured the engineering reports from Agapito and from Lukens (both well known engineers) for further analysis—not just relying on their engineers who used photos taken only from the air. Both Agapito and Lukens drew their conclusions based on the ratios of potassium versus lithium in the production process, and determined how much potassium had to be stored based on the lithium production numbers which were documented in Chemetall Foote's tax returns.

Also, it would have been helpful if they had addressed Chemetall Foote Corp. with the question, *"Why are you importing large amounts of lithium from your Chilean mine to Silver Peak, and are you salting the ponds? "*

U.S. Magnesium, who was also providing salts containing potassium to Silver Peak, was owned by Ira Rennert. Rennert was convicted in 2015 of looting his own company of $118,200,000, during those same years to fund the construction of his mansion on Long Island. This does not speak well of the ethical culture of that now defunct corporate player.

After the whistle blower claim in 2010, Paul is still under Federal Seal for some information.

David Versus Goliath

On October 20, 2014, the BLM put out a news release in Reno, Nevada as follows:

> "*The Bureau of Land Management (BLM), Nevada is seeking interested parties with the means to buy and process approximately 5.5 metric tons of salt. The salt is a byproduct of more than four decades of lithium carbonate processing done by Rockwood Lithium, formerly Chemetall Foote Corporation. The salt consists of approximately 70 percent sodium chloride and 19 percent potassium chloride mechanically scraped from evaporative ponds used in lithium mining. Both salts may be marketable, but must first be processed to a higher percentage of sodium and/or potassium to be marketable. The stockpile of salts also contains lithium at approximately ½ % of the total volume. The lithium is the property of Rockwood.*"

On October 29, 2014, the BLM rejected Paul's potassium permit in its entirety, on the basis that the Patented Lands is now a "Known Leasing Area" for potassium and, therefore, there are no permits allowed to prospect for potassium. So, he has no specified rights to prospect and must go out to bid with all other bidders – no accounting for his application filed in 1989, or the misplacing of the permits and then later finding them again, etc.

After all these years of work and attempted negotiations with Chemetall Foote and Rockwood Corporation, the corporations are left with a lithium mine where they do not owe any royalties to the Federal Government or to the State of Nevada and, Paul Barnes, Jr. is left with a drawer full of permit and legal fee receipts, and no rights to any minerals at Silver Peak, Nevada.

Paul writes on October 25, 2014, to the Bureau of Land Management:

> *"I write to you regarding the announcement concerning the stockpiles at Silver Peak. My position on this matter is that I am potentially entitled to a preference right lease on all potassium and associated secondary minerals stockpiled from May 1, 1989, the date my first application was received…..There is no one else that has pending applications on the Patented Lands and because of this fact it can be easily determined that these stockpiled materials had to come from the areas that I have under application……It was determined in 1989 by the BLM that my permit application was suspended prior to the 1991 settlement. BLM claims they sent me this decision, however after requesting a copy I have never received one. I have only received what appears to be an internal draft of a letter. When the BLM contacted me in 2007 to inquire if I was still interested in the permit application and the stockpiles, I said yes……Why my application was not introduced into the lawsuit or why it did not become a part of the settlement agreement I do not know. It appears that it is, as I was told by the BLM, that it was misplaced.'….Considering the above, I hereby request a stay on the 'expressions of interest,' and any competitive sales or competitive leases as published on the BLM website."*

On February 10, 2015, Paul filed an appeal with the Department of Interior regarding the last denial of his potassium permit and asked for a stay, so the BLM would not continue advertising these leases until there was a ruling on Paul's appeal. The conclusion of the appeal reads:

"Barnes concludes that the Board must reverse BLM's decision, since the

decision has the potential to continue perpetrating an even more egregious injustice on the citizens of the State of Nevada and the United States."

The ruling on the appeal is still pending. The Decision should be rendered in 2017, but the stay was denied. The Interior Board of Land Appeals has stated in the denial of the stay, *"...Barnes has shown a likelihood of success on the merits of his appeal..."* Therefore, the bidding for the potassium leases is on hold, and the bidding process must not go forward pending the decision on Paul's appeal to the Department of Interior.

Ants must crawl; owls must hoot; horses must run; roosters must crow; and corporations must make money – no holds barred – this is how economies operate.

However, citizens pay taxes to governments, so that governments will protect their collective interests. Minerals are not renewable – once taken, they do not regenerate – or, if they do, it takes eons for it to happen. Therefore, governments must be proactive with their checks and balances when monitoring these corporations, or the citizens who pay the taxes suffer by loss of revenue to the collective pot. This loss of revenue results in less money for social services and the education of children. Governments must be fair and vigilant on behalf of their good citizens.

Potassium, with an atomic symbol of "K," is a vital element for plant growth, as plants use potassium to make proteins. Therefore, potassium's best usage is fertilizer, as well as clean energy possibilities based on new technology that is being explored. Potassium is a mineral which can heal the earth. It can be used in soil remediation, which is a huge issue in the production of food, and, in turn, can positively affect world hunger.

Paul Barnes Jr. is described by his wife, Nancy, as a true champion of mankind, a warrior with imagination and altruism. Paul Barnes Jr. would use his rightly owned potassium for the greater good. He would find the best usage of the mineral and would make certain that it got to the very best end user. In the process, he would pay the State of Nevada and the Federal Government all taxes and royalties due.

As a native Nevadan, I put my gamblin' money on Paul Barnes Jr. As a State, we have a better chance of a noble outcome with Paul Barnes, Jr. in charge of our potassium than with a multi-national corporation who can only read a bottom line. Because, in reality, this is all that corporations are designed to do. Tin men are not designed with a heart. Chemetall Foote Corp. is domiciled in Kings Mountain, North Carolina. Rockwood Holdings Co. is domiciled in Princeton, New Jersey, and Albemarle Corporation, the current owner of Silver Peak, is located in Charlotte, North Carolina.

Silver Peak, Nevada is a location where these corporations can make money, but not a place where they will make any substantial investment in the future. Their management cannot be expected to care about the quality of education or health care in Nevada – they don't live here, never have, and never will. They will be funding the symphony and all day kindergarten in their own States – not in Nevada.

Nevada has been raped and pillaged by mining corporations from the discovery of gold and silver at the Comstock in 1864 until the present day. The citizens of Nevada deserve better. And it is up to our elected officials to correctly regulate the mining industry; to create the necessary laws for these "out-of-state" corporations to thrive in our mineral-rich environment; but also to pay their correct dues for the non-renewable resources that they are removing from our land. Moreover, it is up to us citizens to elect public officials who have the tenacious courage to stand up to these corporations at the legislature.

Paul Barnes and Nancy Good live a quiet life in a desert community on the edge of Death Valley, not far from China

Lake, where Paul was born – once a desert rat, always a desert rat! Their lives are filled with family gatherings with their children, Jennifer, Brooke, and step-children, Matt and Theresa; music, art, love and gratitude for one another and for the wonderful life they have been given. But don't count Paul Barnes Jr. out, if continued fighting for his potassium claim is required, as this is his legacy. Paul Barnes Sr. and Clyde Keegel are watching.

Paul T Barnes Jr.

Quote

"Wild honey smells of freedom
The dust - of sunlight
The mouth of a young girl, like a violet
But gold - smells of nothing."

Anna Akhmatova

JORDAN HALE

Nevada Miner

The Silver State Turns to Gold

"You can make a run for the border,
Try to hide at the hole in the wall,
But don't you know your arms
Are aching to hold her,
And cowboy, even though you're riding tall,
You're riding for a fall."

Jordan Hale croons his favorite Chris Ledoux tune as he drives the two lane highway from his home in Spring Creek to Elko. It's 3:00 A.M. and pitch black. No, Jordan is not on his way home from a night out on the town; Jordan Hale is on his way to work. He gets up at 2:45 A.M. fourteen days per month; cooks himself bacon and eggs; feeds the dogs and gets ready for a very long day at work – a day that will really make you think next time you leave for your job.

Spring Creek, a ranching area in the northeastern part of Nevada, is 22 minutes from Elko. It is home to Jordan, his wife, Jessica, and their three small children, three horses, one pony and four dogs. This is not a family designed for city living. Elko only has a population of 18,000, but the Hale family needs more open space than Elko can offer, so they live in near-by Spring Creek. Jordan is a weekend cowboy and a rodeo competitor. Jessica also competes, and their oldest daughter, Austin, age four, is waiting in the wings. She must wait until she turns five to compete, per rodeo regulations – darn!

But this is not a story about a cowboy. This is a story about a Nevada miner, mining for gold on the "Carlin Trend." Jordan Hale is on his way to Elko to meet up with ten other miners who work on his shift at the "Chukar" mine owned by Newmont Mining Corp. The miners converge at a designated parking lot, park their trucks and pile into several highway vans provided by their employer, SMD (Small Mine Development, LLC.)

Of the ten miners—well, there is a distinction that needs to be made here—four are miners and seven are either muckers or loaders. I will be referring to all of them as miners, which is a generic term for ease in communication. Three of these miners reside full time in Elko and the others actually live in other states—Montana and Utah—and they commute every other week into Elko for their seven days on, returning to their homes for the seven days off.

They live in hotel rooms in Elko or they rent rooms in private homes. There is no "man camp" or barracks on the Carlin Trend. These men are bonafide "tramp miners." The miners must leave Elko by 4:20 A.M. – still dark – as they must travel 23 miles to Carlin on Highway 80, and then about six miles up to the entrance of the "Chukar" mine.

The town of Elko lies along the route of the historic California Trail, which is now Highway 80 running east/west across the northern third of Nevada. It straddles the Humboldt River and is the largest city for 130 miles in all directions, and, I emphasize the word "all." Elko was settled in 1868, when the Central Pacific railroad was laid across northern Nevada – part of the First Transcontinental Railroad built from California to Utah.

I would call this area of Nevada "high, high desert." The elevation is 5,066 feet, and it sits at 41 degrees latitude. The climate is semi-arid, with an average of 24 days per year that do not top freezing, 198 nights with freezing lows and an annual precipitation average of 9.89 inches. The growing season is short – (No kidding!)

In other words folks, plant all the flowers and vegetables you want, but they are "go'in ta freeze!" I asked Jordan if he liked Elko, *"Hell no; I hate it; there aren't any trees."* It's damn cold in Elko—wide open plains—too far from a shopping mall. But they've got gold, and lots of it!

Carlin, 23 miles west of Elko, also on Highway 80, is the gateway to the largest gold mines in North America. It's a small town of 2,368 people, which exists primarily to support the mines. Nevada, known commonly as "The Silver State," was given this name shortly after being admitted to the Union in 1864, since silver was the primary ore mined for many years.

Today, Nevada should really be renamed the "Gold State!" It is home to the Carlin Trend, not only the most prolific producer of gold in North America, but also the second largest known gold strike in the world. The Carlin Trend was formed when a tectonic crustal block collided with the North American Plate. Hot springs formed due to pressure and temperature along the suture zone, pushing dissolved minerals toward the surface of the earth.

Geologists call the Carlin type deposits "disseminated gold," meaning "spread throughout." The gold appears in the Paleozoic limy sediments as microscopic flecks which can't be seen with the naked eye, and were, thus, beyond discovery by the early prospectors. It is low grade ore but with a heck of a volume—the trend is a belt of gold deposits about 50 miles wide and 40 miles long.

Initially, the gold was mined from open pits and still is in some areas. However, in 1994, some mining companies began to move underground to capture deposits of higher grade ore "down dip" from the open pits. Also, many of the pits were already as deep as they could be dug, due to the size of the circumference of the pit. Many new techniques have been pioneered at the Carlin Trend. One in particular is "cyanide-heap-leaching," used to efficiently separate the gold from the surrounding sediment. This technique, refined in Nevada, is now used worldwide.

5:00 A.M – The eleven miners arrive in the highway vans at the gate leading into the Chukar mine where they pass a large white sign with red painted letters reading, *"Absolutely no drugs, firearms, or alcohol on this property. Vehicles are subject to search."* They proceed through security at the gate and drive a short distance to "the dry" (a building with locker rooms and showers) where the men "digger up" (change from street clothes into their mining over-alls or "diggers.") They each have a backpack with their lunch and beverages for the day—there is no Mc Donalds or Starbucks underground at the Chukar mine. The miner's street clothes and wallets are secured in assigned lockers.

At this point, all eleven miners pile into the "dirty vans" and start driving the long circular road down to the bottom of the pit where they park at the north portal, the northern entrance to the Chukar mine tunnels. There is also another portal at the south end of the pit.

5:30 A.M. – Dawn is breaking as the 11 miners enter the small offices at the bottom of the pit to study the maps of the tunnels, do the "pass-downs," load the tractors, "clock in," and "brass in." The geologists have laid out the scope of work in each tunnel off the north portal far into 2019, and each day the miners work with their foreman, using the geologist's maps to determine their mining goals for that day.

At about that same time, 5:30 A.M., the night shift, (also 11 men) are exiting from the north portal. Each miner meets with his counter-part on the night shift to do the "pass down," – the night shift miner tells the day shift miner exactly what he accomplished on the night shift; where he left off; any problems he encountered, or any problems that the day shift might encounter; and gives a detailed explanation of exactly what equipment the day shift miner must take into the mine with him. This information is vitally important, as the day shift miner will be traveling another half hour underground to get to the "headers" where he will work.

If a miner is caught without the correct equipment, it means a full hour will be lost in that day's work while he backtracks to the portal to get what he needs and then traces his steps back to the header. Since the men are paid an hourly wage plus bonus for production, many a black eye has been received due to an inadequate or inaccurate "pass down."

After the "pass-down", the miner clocks-in and, more importantly, he also moves his brass piece from the "out" board over onto a hook on the "in" board, to show that he is entering the underground country. A forgotten "clock-in" could affect your paycheck, but a forgotten "brass-in" could cost lives.

The moving of the brass pieces from the "in" board to the "out" board, and visa-versa, has been used in every underground mine since the 1860's—and maybe before. It has proven to be the most reliable means of tracking who is or who is not inside the mine at any given moment.

The miners have done the "pass-downs," and now the 11 day-shift miners start loading the tractors with the needed equipment for the day's work, as they will not be coming out of the tunnels until their shift is over about 5:00 P.M. The 11 very tired and dirty night-shift miners clock-out, brass-out, and now pull themselves up into the "dirty vans" for their drive to the top of the pit to shower and change at "the dry" for the last leg of their journey back to Elko to dinner and a soft bed.

Jordan Finds His Passion

I first met Jordan Hale on July 15, 2016, at the Windmill Café outside of Alamo, Nevada. We decided the Windmill was half way between Panaca, where the Hale family was visiting with Jessica's parents, and Boulder City, where I live. We agreed to have lunch together and for me to interview Jordan about his life and his work as a miner.

Jordan Bruce Hale was born Feb.1, 1990, in Las Vegas, the son of Bruce and Kathy Hale. His grandparents living in Pioche are Frank Lloyd, Ann Hartley Lloyd, Sherri Devlin, and his step-grandfather, Jim Devlin.

Jordan attended the Pioche elementary school and Lincoln County High School, as did his parents, as did his grandparents, as did I, and as did my father. Although very far apart in age, Jordan and I have a lot in common; we've walked the same walk (literally and figuratively). Things don't change much in Lincoln County.

In high school his favorite subjects were welding and auto mechanics. Football, baseball and rodeo club filled his extra-curricular hours. The latter became attractive to Jordan due to the related attractiveness of the cowgirls in the club!

After graduation and the senior trip, Jordan loaded everything he owned into the back of his pick up and headed to Las Vegas. His dad was a member of the Pipe Fitters union, and Jordan aspired to join his father in the same trade. However, after 18 months, the great recession hit Las Vegas with an atomic-powered wrench, leaving no construction jobs to be had – union or non-union. There were no jobs.

Jordie moved back to Pioche and took a side job for about six months renewing a portal drift at an old Pioche mine. The job was a "backyard" type of operation with poor equipment, poor safety practices and was accompanied by several near misses. Jordan got a very good taste of the downside of mining – what not to do in and or near a mine, especially an old mine.

After six months, a buddy in Utah told Jordan that his employer needed help at a Dude Ranch on Zion Mountain in Utah. He signed on and initially helped with the Dude Ranch, but later was transferred to the "buffalo herding" department. This ranch owned 100 buffalo which were being used as a tourist attraction. So, every couple of days, the cowboys had to herd the 100 head of buffalo up close to the fences, so the tourists could take pictures. Jordan shared with me that, *"Buffalo do not like horses!"*

While on that job, Jordan learned from an older cowboy in the area how to shoe horses and how to do leather work. Unfortunately, the other cowboys in the "herding buffalo" department had a falling out with management, and Jordan was once again out of a job.

Upon contacting some family friends in Winnemucca, Jordan decided to try his luck with the job market in central Nevada. He landed a welding job with a small company who made agricultural and rodeo fences – a job tailor made for Jordan. They worked mainly around Big Fork and Kalispell, Montana – a good gig for Jordan, *"It was lots of fun!"*

One day while nursing a cold beer in a Winnemucca saloon, Jordan started talking with a local who was holding up the bar. The guy started talking about "jacklegs." Jordan exclaimed, *"I can run jacklegs!"* Of course Jordan could run a jackleg. Jordan was raised in Pioche, Nevada, one of the first silver mining boom-towns in the State. He has one step-grandfather and at least two great grand-fathers who were Pioche miners.

He remembered seeing the jacklegs and drills in his step-grandfather's garage – he knew how to balance them and how they ran. When he was 13, Jordan desperately wanted to enter the jackleg mining competition on Labor Day in Pioche, but was told that he was too young and lightweight to enter.

Undaunted, Jordan discovered that he could enter the team competition by partnering with an adult. He teamed up with his dad and they took 1st place. He then teamed up with an older miner, a friend of the family, Floyd Burns, and they took 2nd place! Mining was in his blood, so when offered a job with SMD at the "Fire Creek" mine, Jordan jumped at the chance. He hired on in October of 2011—Jordan was 21 years old. There were only three miners working at that mine, so Jordan needed to learn fast—very fast.

Usually, a newly hired young guy would work at least one to two years as a "nipper," (a helper), or as a truck driver. Often times, a newly hired employee can work for up to five years before being promoted to a miner. But this mine was short handed, and they needed to accelerate the process at Fire Creek; so Jordan, now a fully developed, strong man, was promoted to miner after only three weeks as a nipper and had to sink or swim. Jordan's mother, Kathy, summed it up, *"As soon as Jordan went underground, he was a very happy man."*

Later he was moved to Leeville mine and then to Chukar. Since Jordan has worked in three mines in as many years, he qualifies as a "tramp" miner. He also confirmed that there are so many miners needed in northern Nevada, due to the large number of individual mines on the Carlin Trend, that a miner can easily quit three times and return before management would say anything. The tramp mining life-style is alive and well, surviving after 150 years in Nevada.

Rubber Tire Mining

Art Hartley was Jordan's great-grandfather on his mother's side. He and his wife, Edna, hailed from Kansas where they owned a small service station. It was the mid-1930's – the middle of the great depression, and times were beyond tough. Art heard that miners were making good money working in the mines in Nevada. He and Edna talked it over and decided that they just didn't have much to lose, so why not take a chance. They sold the service station and one cow, packed their few belongs and headed west to Pioche, Nevada.

Art went to work for the Pan American mine, an incline shaft mine, in 1936, and Edna cooked for the miners. Art later transferred to the "Prince" mine in Caselton, located on the back side of Pioche's famous Treasure Hill. In time, Art, a true entrepreneur, purchased a service station in Pioche with a partner, Lewis Scott, but continued to work one shift each day at the mine and a second shift at the service station. He did this for years, but was eventually able to quit the mine and run the service station full time—later building and operating a small motel as well, making a respectable living for his wife and three daughters—one of which is Ann Hartley Lloyd, Jordan's maternal grandmother.

6:00 A.M.—the eleven miners have "clocked-in" and "brassed-in" and are now loading the tractor (a small tractor designed to fit the tunnels) with all of the supplies needed for their work this shift.

William Lloyd was Jordan's great-great grandfather, a Welch miner, who had emigrated from Wales in 1879 to work in the mines in Pioche. He worked at the Boston mine, the Silver Peak, the Mezzappi, the No. 1 and the Yuba.

William's son, Daniel, was born in 1889 in Pioche and was mucking for his dad at the Pacific tunnel by the age of 10. After reaching adulthood, Daniel became a hoisting engineer and a blacksmith at various Pioche mines.

Daniel's son, Frank, broke the family tradition when he became a policeman and married Jordan's grandmother, Ann Hartley.

Jordan is qualified as a miner, and he can do all of the mining jobs, which include drilling, setting charges, driving trucks, mucking and bolting. However, for the past three years, he has been operating the bolters and installing bolts exclusively. To bring us up to date with current mining procedures, timber and timber sets are no longer used in mines to hold up tunnels. The tunnels and the headers are supported by large steel rods, commonly referred to in the mines as bolts. It is Jordan's full time job on every shift to install bolts, and the safety of the tunnels truly does rest on his abilities to do his job correctly – there is no room for having a bad day and producing shoddy work.

So, the miners have determined the exact number and size of bolts needed to support the exact number of headers to be constructed on this shift. The selected bolts are either 16' X 16", or 16' X 18", or 16' X 28", depending on the size of the header under construction.

The 16' bolt will take two hours to install.
The 18' bolt will take two and one-half hours to install.
The 28' bolt will take three and one-half hours to install.

Jordan must plan every hour underground in advance, in order to install the needed bolts in each header so that the miners can move forward, removing new ground in the tunnel according to the geologists' plans. Any miner that holds up the process, costs everyone time and money; and, of course, becomes instantly unpopular with his "*pardners.*"

The tractor is outfitted with a carousel which holds all of the bolts and will seat six men, as will the Kubota. The vehicles are loaded; the miners have their hard hats, respirators, goggles, backpacks, and all of the mining tools needed for the next eleven hours of hard work. They are ready to enter the portal and to drive 35 mph for another half hour through the maze of tunnels to arrive at their destination. There is one main tunnel know as "the main," and then there are tunnels going off in every direction from that point. The portals are 15' X 15' and the tunnels are all from 15' to 18' high.

In 1864, most miners were traveling on foot or on a donkey, with no resources to afford a ride in a hired wagon; and they were carrying their equipment on their backs or tied to the side of the faithful donkey. Now, mining is all "*rubber tire*" mining – mining from the cabs of the trucks. The miner is directing machines which do the bulk of the work.

Mining in 1936 by Roscoe Wilkes, Jr.

Roscoe Wilkes, Jr., my dad, writes of his experience being hired on at the Number 1 mine in Pioche as an 18 year old in 1936. It's interesting to compare his experiences alongside Jordan's.

> *"My peers were amazed, surprised and perhaps even startled. 'Roscoe Wilkes is going down in the mine!' Until that time, no 18 year old, recent high school graduate had been known to work underground in the mine. It was hard work and dirty; considered by some to be unhealthy and dangerous. Why then did I do it? I was tired of being poor. It paid $3.75 a day, and I hoped to overcome the odds and go to college.*
>
> *"On Monday with my street shoes in the basket and my clothes on the hooks all pulled up to the ceiling of the change room by a chain and pulley, and in the worst clothes I could find, 'my diggers,' I was ready for the descent down the shaft. I had been issued a hard hat to which I attached my carbide lamp. Lunch kit and leather-lined gloves in hand, I stepped into the skip with five other workers..."*
>
> *"In the hoist house the hoistman sat behind a huge drum around which were wound layers of one-inch diameter cable. With levers he could guide the drum to wind up or unwind the cable. The cable extended from the drum outside to the top of the gallows frame, on the very top of which was the sheave (pronounced by the miners 'shiv') wheel. The cable fits in the sheave wheel and extends down to the skip. The hoistman could lower the skip down 1200 feet to the mine's bottom from the surface, or stop it anywhere in between as might be needed. He was controlled by bell signals given by the skip tender—one*

bell for up, two bells for down and other bells for other purposes. A good hoistman drew great respect from the miners who, of necessity, rode the skip.

"Getting off the skip at the 1200 foot level, one was in a large underground room. A bit of dampness was felt, and the air had a different smell, not unpleasant but different. The 1200 foot station was the hub, the center of underground activity where many things were stored, and was home base for the electric motor and numerous ore cars, where the ore was loaded on the skip for the trip to the surface. During the shift when the miners were working, the skip ran nonstop taking care of many chores.

"Leaving the 1200 foot station, the workers, walking single file, started the trip west, down the 1200 drift (tunnel). That walk, between or alongside the very narrow gage tracks, continued for a substantial distance, maybe one eighth of a mile to what was known as the 11/7 raise. There, the workers, three at a time, entered a smaller skip and were hoisted upward to the 950 foot level where another short walk took place back to the stopes where the actual mining took place.

"The trip from the surface to the stopes consumed the better part of an hour. When arriving at their work place, those who smoked sat down for their smoke and bit of rest. When the work shift was over the same trip in reverse was necessary taking the better part of another hour. The mining law provided for an 8-hour day, meaning that miners could not be kept underground for more than an 8-hour shift. These factors and a few others made working in a mine a good job. The work day went fast.

"A team consisted of three people, a miner and two muckers. The miner who earned 50 cents a day extra was the leader. He did the machine drilling, handled the dynamite and the blasting, etc. The muckers had three tools, a pick, a shovel and a wheelbarrow between them. First off, the miner, alone with a metal bar in hand, would gingerly enter the work area tapping the back (roof) with a metal bar. The sound gave him his

answers. A solid ringing sound established that the back was solid. A dullish, non-ringing sound indicated loose rock slabs overhead which, for the safety of the workers, would need to be barred down or timbered before work could be started.
"If the loose back couldn't be barred down the timbermen were called. They would promptly appear with stulls, wood plates and wedges. A stull would be measured and cut for correct length and with a plate top and bottom placed from floor to back would be tightly wedged into place. A stull is a log, telephone pole size in diameter and 8 to 10 feet long. When properly placed it takes the weight and protects those working from falling rocks or boulders."

These stulls have now been replaced with the metal bolts that Jordan installs – same technique, but Jodan can install the bolts with a machine and they are stronger and will never rot.

Roscoe continues, *"Deeming the work area safe, the miner would commence the setting up of his drilling equipment and start his drilling. The jackhammer sound in the tight quarters was nearly unbearable. Conversation was impossible unless he shut the lyner (a special jackhammer) down to change to a longer piece of drilling steel.*
"The muckers, shirt off and muck pile wet down, with head down and ass up, would attack the muck pile with intense vigor. The muck pile consisted of what the previous shift had blasted down from the 'face' (wall)......"
"Wheelbarrows in 1936 did not have rubber tires. The wheels were spokes surrounded by a metal plate. Hitting the slightest rock could upset the heavy load. The answer – we laid down 2 X 12 boards, end to end, and created a path for the steel wheel. It was necessary, however, to stay on the path.
"Mucking was either 'off the rough' or 'off the boards'. Mucking off the rough occurred when the previous shift failed to or couldn't lay down the boards. The blasted-down ore was

therefore on the mine floor, usually uneven and rough. Only a round pointed shovel could be used. Extra effort was needed and the work was considerably harder and slower than mucking off boards......."

"During the mid-shift lunch break the workers from several stopes would gather, sit on the boards with backs to the wall, eat their lunch and spill forth with discussions and stories of subject matters in abundance and extraordinarily varied....

"After lunch with often most of the work completed things were calmer. With his drilling completed, the miner having his 'round' done, loading the holes commenced. Often the miner would have drilled nine holes in the face, three in a row (uppers); three in a row (mid-level) and three in a row (lower level) called lifters.

"Armed with numerous sticks of dynamite, blasting caps, a quantity of fuse and a long, wooden tamping stick, he started. Each hole was loaded in much the same way. One at a time three or four sticks of dynamite were slid into the hole and gently but firmly pushed tight against the end of the hole. I could say the dynamite was 'tamped in,' but 'pushed' in was a better description. One handled 'powder' with care. At about the halfway mark in the hole, a stick of dynamite containing a blasting cap on the end of a length of fuse was very carefully and tenderly pushed against that already there. Lastly, three or four more sticks of dynamite were pushed and tightened into the hole. It was now fully loaded.

"It should be noted that the length of the fuse on all nine holes was different. The blast of each hole was in sequence. Not all exploded at once. The time between each blast was determined by the length of the fuse. At the appropriate time the miner would order, 'Everybody out, I'm spittin' (lighting) the fuses.' Everyone would depart for a spot 50 yards or so away and congregate. Shortly, the miner, having spit the fuses, would join them. As the blasts occurred they were counted. Nine holes meant nine blasts.

Roscoe concludes, *"With the blasting completed the trek back to the surface started. Arriving on top, it was remove the wet, filthy diggers, enjoy a hot shower, back into regular street clothes, head for home and look forward to payday and those big bucks like $22.50 for the week."*

Jordan Mines "Gyppo"

It is 6:30 A.M. (2016), and Jordan, our modern miner, has arrived at the first designated header. He must check the ventilation with an instrument and note the results on a paper form; he must check a second time to make sure all of the needed equipment is on the tractor and note this on a separate form. Lastly, he needs to check each piece of equipment to make sure nothing is broken or malfunctioning, and this must also be noted on a third form.

The muckers must clean the stopes from the blasting by the prior shift and then leave. Jordan then steps in and starts to install the needed bolts; if installing a 16' X 16" bolt, he will be at it for two hours. Jordan will call for the loader to clean out the header again, and then he will call for a driller to drill holes in the header for the next round of explosives to be placed for blasting. Unlike the mining of 1936, no blasting will take place until the end of the shift, when all but two of the miners have already "brassed-out."

The driller, using 42 mm. drill bits, will drill a hole into the ceiling of the tunnel at the location of the noted header. The bolter, Jordan, will then stand the metal bolt in place to be mechanically pushed into the hole. The top of the bolt is fitted with a flange, which, when fully in place, will mechanically be driven to expand in all directions into the rocky formation above the tunnel. Enough of these bolts placed correctly will hold up the back tunnels without any timbers. This process makes the tunnels safer than if timbered and provides more space in the tunnels for the tractors.

The Chukar mine, Jordan's place of employment for the past few years, is owned by Newmont Corporation, founded in 1921, and headquartered in Colorado. This corporation is one of the world's largest gold producers with 28,000 employees in the U.S., Australia, New Zealand, Peru, Indonesia and Ghana. Newmont controls 2.8 million acres in Nevada, which is responsible for one third of their worldwide gold production. They operate 11 surface mines, 8 underground mines and 13 processing facilities, which are responsible for processing three million ounces of gold annually.

Sometimes a large corporation like Newmont will handle the mining operation themselves, but much of the time they will sub-contract operations out to a smaller contractor. Often the smaller sub-contractor will be able to reduce expenses and increase the efficiency of production, as well as spreading the risks and liabilities between the two entities.

In the case of the Chukar mine, Newmont has sublet operations to SMD Corporation. SMD was founded in 1982 by Ron Guill, a mining engineer who graduated from the Mackay School of Mines at the University of Nevada at Reno. SMD is Jordan's employer. They have an exemplary record of engineering newer and better ways of mining, many of which are now used around the world. Worthy of mention are the following innovations:

- The use of 100% cemented backfill in underhand cut and fill mining – used in challenging ground conditions (bad dirt!).
- Installing portals in open pit mines.
- Utilizing mechanized bolting.
- Using wet shotcrete for ground support.
- Installing diesel particulate filters and other innovations to allow diesel tractors to run safely underground.

12:00 noon – Jordan Hale is stringing wire and installing bolts. He must keep the bolter running constantly to guarantee meeting quotas. He pauses in the cab of the tractor to eat a sandwich and drink some water but, rest assured, the bolter is still running. I asked Jordan if he has trouble keeping his energy up for this long shift. He says that he used to take energy pills, but had been over-using them, causing side effects, so now he just chews tobacco when he needs a lift. Says, *"It keeps me sane."*

The miners wear respirators with filters. The ventilation is very good in "the main" as there are several vent shafts, but it is very difficult to ventilate the headers. They do use large blowers, but the temperature can be 65 degrees in the main and 118 degrees in the header.

Jordan finishes lunch and gets out of the tractor to spread wires and hook up another bolt. He activates a pump which causes the top of the bolt to spiral outwards, providing the wide support needed to stabilize the "back".

2:00 p.m.—Time for the next bolt. Jordan is very proud to work for SMD. It's a good company which is designed for speed. By September of 2016 the Chukar miners were already 10,000 ounces of gold over their annual goal. It's a good team.

The teams of miners are paid hourly, but also have a production bonus with SMD. The bonus is sizeable, which provides high motivation for the team to work together. They get a bonus for tonnage of ore taken out, and also a footage bonus for pushing the tunnels ahead to uncover new country. A fully classified miner gets 100% of the bonus; a mucker would get 40 to 45% of the bonus; and a truck driver might get 20% of the bonus. A fully classified miner could make $150,000 per year, if the production stays at maximum level. SMD also offers a 401K retirement plan, medical, dental and vision insurance, paid vacation and paid holidays.

Jordan Hale, a fast and efficient miner, is working "gyppo" as did his predecessor, Jack Brown.

3:00 p.m. – time for Jordan to move to the last header. As the afternoon progresses, quitting time seems within reach, bringing Jordan's thoughts to Jessica and the kids at home.

The Miner Takes a Wife

Jordan met Jessica Dojaquez in Panaca when he was in High School and Jessica was in Middle School – she was 13 years old. Three years later, Jordan was mining for SMD and living in a camp trailer in Elko. On a return trip to Lincoln County to attend the wedding of one of his buddies, he ran into Jessica and they started talking….and talking….and talking. Soon, Jordan was driving to Panaca to date Jessica on his days off twice every month – about a five hour drive each way. They were star-crossed for sure. There is simply no doubt about it.

What can I say about Jessica? Well, it was sunny, with scattered, cotton-ball shaped, white clouds on Mount Olympus the day the Gods convened for their monthly meeting – Zeus presiding, of course. Number three on the agenda that day was, *"Should we send a young goddess to earth to mate with an earthling and give birth?"* The vote was taken, and it was a unanimous *"yes"* vote. The young goddess, Jessica, was sent flying to earth on a great black steed to mate with the earthling, Jordan, and to give birth to babies, who would represent the Gods and, in time, work for peace on earth.

Jessica is beautiful with her long, silky black hair; and she is mature beyond her years (an old soul). She is earth mother to her three children, Austin, Oakley and Tuff, and they will all be eternally connected to the nether world through their horses. And, best of all, the earthling, Jordan, knows that being married to a goddess comes with great responsibility – and, he is up to the task!

Brassing Out

I asked Jordan if he is ever scared while working underground. He said *"no,"* that the only time he was ever really scared on the job was the day when his boss was rushing him from the mine to the hospital, after they had been notified that Jessica's water had broken and baby "Oakley" would be arriving any time. Jordan says, *"my boss was driving so fast, I thought I might die on the highway before we got to the hospital."*

5:00 p.m. – The shifter tractor has arrived to pick up Jordan and the other 10 miners. However, it is Jordan and one other miner's turn to light fuses, so they wait until they are radio'd that everyone else has "brassed–out" except them. The last two guys light the fuses and drive their tractor to the next header. As they light the second fuses, they hear the blast from the first fuses – and on they go until all the fuses are lit.

5:30 to 5:45 p.m. – Jordan is back to the portal; he has "brassed-out" and it's time to "pass-down" to the night-shift bolter, being careful to not forget any information that might be useful for his pardner on night-shift. The 11 miners, completely black with underground dirt from the Chukar mine, pour into the "dirty vans" and drive to the top of the pit. Depending on time of year, it is often as dark as it was when they entered the portal that morning.

6:00 to 6:10 p.m. – The miners go into "the dry" where they will take off the dirty diggers, shower and dress in their street clothes, which for Jordan means western shirt, Levi's, boots and gold and silver cowboy belt buckle. At the end of the 7th shift, Jordan takes his three sets of diggers to a laundromat in Elko, which has invested in a commercial washing machine to service the miner's diggers – and in Elko, that's a lot of diggers. Jordan will not take them home, as often there will be parts of explosives in the pockets – what happens in the mine, stays in the mine – or in the laundromat!

    6:30 to 6:45 p.m. – The miners alight into the highway vans and drive back to Elko, arriving about 7:00 p.m. If it is the end of the 7th shift, the miners may (or actually, pretty much for sure) go for a few beers and maybe a few whiskeys, to boot. The intensity of their work and the intensity of their partnerships, makes letting off steam once in a while a necessity – another thing that hasn't changed in 150 years! If it is after the shift of the 4th, 5th or 6th day, Jordan will be driving on to Spring Creek in his own pickup. He will arrive home to greet Jessica and the kids, as if he has had a long day at the office. He plays with the kids, eats dinner, feeds horses, and goes to bed between 8:30 and 9:00 p.m., as he will have to arise at 2:45 a.m. again the next morning to fry bacon and eggs and start over.

    After the 7th shift, however, all of the 11 miners will have seven glorious days off to spend with their families. Jordan will probably drive with Jessica and the kids to Pioche or to Panaca to see family and maybe to ride a buckin' bronc or two! Depending on the time of year, Jordan and Jessica may lay down a few traps for bobcats or coyotes – a hobby that they enjoy doing together. Some years when the fur market is up, they can pick up an extra $1000 or more. Lately, the fur market has been low, and Jessica has used the hides to make some fabulous men's gloves.

    Pioche miner, Darrel Free, now deceased, reports during his oral history interview in 1992:

Q. *"Where do you find the most lion in this area?"*
A. *"The lion live on deer, primarily, so they follow the deer from the summer range to the winter range."*
Q. *"Where's their summer range?"*
A. *"In the high mountains. They travel along the mountain range. That's the way I've hunted them, across the roads that go over the mountain range."*
Q. *"Which mountains do you hunt the most in?"*
A. *"Probably in Area 23."*

There have been many changes in the way miners remove the ore from the tunnels, but not so much has changed in the lives of the miners. Trapping, hunting, and riding bucking broncos are still favorite pastimes for many miners.

When the miners return after the seven days off, they will go back to the mine on night shift, as the day shift and night shift miners alternate every seven days. Being a miner is a good life, and Jordan loves his job. There is a tactile satisfaction stemming from the art of following carefully thought-out detailed plans which re-arrange mother earth so that her treasures can be used for the greater good. It's a complicated board game of man against nature with a physical component, a mental component, and the added benefit of the dynamics of being part of a closely knit team. It's a band of brothers pitting themselves against Mother Nature each and every shift.

I asked Jordan what he considered to be the qualities of a good miner. His analysis is that it takes a man with physical strength, for sure, but that a good miner must also be disciplined and not *"have any quit in him."* He must have good time control, not be complacent, but also needs to speak up when he feels strongly about a decision to proceed in a certain manner, as some decisions can mean the difference between coming home safely that night or not.

I then asked Jordan how long he planned to mine. He answered quickly, needing no time to think, "*I will mine until I can't mine no more.*" Spoken like a true hard-rock miner of today, as only a miner spawned from 137 years of hard-rock Nevada miners could speak.

Jordan Bruce Hale

ACKNOWLEDGMENTS

How does one thank a deceased parent who gave you life itself, and then was responsible for providing you with all the tools to succeed and the humor and resilience to enjoy the ride? Thank you Dad for taking me with you on weekends in your old green pick-up truck to every abandoned mine and ranch in Lincoln County.

Also, thank you for allowing me to edit the precious stories you wrote during the last years of your life, because it led me to writing about Nevada. How you would have loved to help me with the research for this book, and how much better it would have been if you had. You and Aunt Kathryn, my high-school English teacher (all four years), gave me the tools; and, evidently, I was meant to take it from there.

My dear friend, Bobbi Jo – We met in the first grade. You were on the cutting edge in Lincoln County—you knew everybody and everything about life. If you hadn't taken me under your wing, I would know nothing about men, fashion, or how to tease my hair! And, a special thanks to fellow Nevadans, Linda Faiss and Helen Foley, for taking charge when I landed in Las Vegas.

Thank you, Rebecca Haag, for pouring over my lengthy manuscript on weekends, dotting "i's", crossing "t's", and trimming dangling participles, as well as being a great neighbor!

John L. Smith, your willingness to encourage and help a fledgling Nevada author is noteworthy and a sign of your character and love for Nevada. .

How do you thank a spouse who is willing to take on the job of professional "roadie" for a nerdy wife who has decided late in life to follow a literary-calling. Thank you, Darryl Martin, for a truly magnificent book cover and for listening to me talk endlessly about four Nevada miners and their mines. Books are not written in a vacuum. It takes a village to give them life.

BIBLIOGRAPHY

Barnes, Paul T. Jr. *Correspondence to U.S. Dept of Interior, Dept. of Justice, Office of U.S. Attorney, Bureau of Land Management, Regional Solicitor Pacific Southwest Region:* 11-25-2014

Barnes, Paul T. Jr. *E-mail to Timothy Mc Kenna, V.P. Investor Relations and Comunications, Rockwood Rockwood Holdings, Inc.:* 02-19-2009

Barnes, Paul T. Jr. *Barnes Permit Application on Patented Lands Filed with BLM, Tonopah:* 05-31-1989

Barnes, Paul T. Jr. *Suspension of Permit Listed above:* 11-06-1989

Barnes, Paul T. Jr. *Permit Filed with BLM Covering Patented Lands and Stockpile. NVN.087382:* 2009

Barnes, Paul T. Jr. *Appeal to Dept. of Interior.(Now Pending):* 02-10-2015

Braden, Spruille. *Diplomats and Demagogues- The Memoirs of Spruille Braden:* Arlington House. 1971

Brautigan, Richard. *Trout Fishing in America:* Houghton Mifflin/Seymour Lawrence. 1967

Bureau of Land Management. *Correspondence to Leprechaun Mining and Mineral Co.* 01-17-1989

Bureau of Land Management. *To Chemetall Foote (Land Patent No. 27-89-0018) issued.* 11-25-1988

Chemetall Foote v.s. U.S.Govt. *U.S.- CV –S-89-108 Docket:* 02-07-1989 through 07-12-1991.

Chemetall Foote. *Settlement with U.S. Govt Re: Stockpiled salts*: 06-20-1991

Chemetall Foote. *Application to BLM for Prospecting Permit for Lithium as Locatable.* 06-23-1983

Hall, Shawn. *Ghost Towns and Mining Camps of Southern Nevada:* Arcadia Publishing 2010

Hawley, Charles. *A Kennecott Story (Three Mines, Four Men, and One Hundred Years):* University of Utah Press. 2014

Hopkins, A.D. *Gunfighters of Pioche*: Nevada Magazine. Oct. 1986

Hulse, James W. *The Camp that Came Back – The Combined Metals Reduction Company and the Revival Of Pioche 1912-1958:*

Keegel, Clyde. *Correspondence to Chemetall Foote:* 02/28/1989

Kelley, Lillian. *My Most Memorable Christmas:* Pioche Record (date unknown)

Leprechaun Mining and Mineral Co. V.S. Chemetall Foote. *Settlement Agreement:* 05-01-1993

Lukes, Jerome A. *Correspondence to James L. Wadsworth, esq. Representing Leprechaun Mining and Mineral Co:* 08-03-1992

Mc Cracken, Robert D. *Oral History with Darrel Free:* Lincoln County Town History Project. 03-15-1993

Mc Cracken, Robert D. *Oral History with Merrill Barnum:* Lincoln County Town History Project.03-31-1992 and 07-04-1992

Mc Cracken, Robert D. *Oral History with John Franks:* Lincoln County Town History Project. 02-21-1990 and 02-22-1990

Parcel, Randy. *Correspondence to Crockett of Leprechaun Mining and Mineral Co:* 12-06-1982

Parcel, Randy. *Correspondence to Clyde Keegel of Leprechaun Mining and Mineral Co:* 01-19-1983

Shumway, Corinne Fullerton and Hone, Peggy Draper. *I Dig Pioche:* The Pioche Historical Society

State of Nevada, Inspector of Mines. *Official accident report of the death of John Clayton Brown.* 03-14-1953 through 03-31-1953

Stegner, Wallace. *Angle of Repose:* Doubleday & Company, Inc: 1971

United States of America and the State of Nevada, ex rel. Paul T. Barnes, Jr. v.s. Chemetall Foote Corporation. *Complaint for Violation of Federal False Claims Act (31 U.S.C. 3729 et seq) and Nevda False Claims Act. (Nev. Rev. Stat. 357.01 0 et.seq.):* 06-08-2010

GLOSSARY OF MINING TERMS

BACK: The roof or upper part of any mining cavity.
BRASS-IN: To move a brass piece assigned to a miner from the board showing you are outside the mine to the board showing you are inside the mine. A function which has been used in mines around the world for over 100 years.
COLLAR: A term denoting the mouth of a shaft at the surface. Can be natural rock or lined with a wooden frame or cribbing (timber set).
DIGGERS: Men's overalls which miners wear when mining. Term used for at least 80 years.
DRIFT: An underground horizontal passage lying in or near the length of the ore body.
FACE: The more or less vertical surface of rock exposed by blasting or excavation.
GYPPO: A formula of payment to miners based on individual production rather than "by the hour."
HARD-ROCK-MINING: Prospecting, development and recovery of ores from solid or hard rock, whether from the surface or under-ground.
HITCH: Fracture or dislocation of the ore strata – a geological fault.
HOIST: To raise or lift a mechanical apparatus from lower levels in a mine shaft. The apparatus could carry equipment, ore or miners.
HEADERS: A framing member crossing and supporting the ends of joists, studs or rafters.
LITHIUM: A soft, silver-white metallic element, the lightest of all metals, occurring combined in certain minerals. Symbol: "Li"

LEASABLE MINERALS: Per 1920 Mineral Leasing Act, leasable minerals include oil, gas, geothermal resources, potash, sodium, bituminous rock, phosphates, sulfur and coal. Royalties are paid to U.S. and State governments when these ores are extracted.

LOCATABLE MINERALS: These are minerals not leasable and are managed under the General Mining Law of 1872 and BLM regulations. They are gold, silver, copper and gemstones; and can usually be recognizable one from another. Taxes are paid when the minerals are sold.

PARD: Informal way of addressing a partner or friend.

PAY DIRT: Soil, gravel or ore that can be mined profitably. Term can be used loosely for any source of success or wealth.

POTASSIUM: A silvery, white metallic element that oxidizes rapidly in the air and whose compounds are used as fertilizer and special hard glasses. Symbol "K"

PORTAL: The rock face entrance to a horizontal underground passageway, which is often protected by a wooden structure (a timber set).

TO PROSPECT: To search or explore a region for metals.

PROSPECTOR: A person who searches or explores a region looking for a metal deposit that has economic value (pay dirt).

RAISE: A vertical underground passage excavated upward for the purpose of connecting adjacent levels.

SHAFT: A vertical or nearly vertical opening (rectangle in shape) excavated downward into the earth from the surface to aid movement of personnel, equipment, recovered ore, and for ventilation and water removal.

SHEAVE: (pronounced "shiv") – A rotating, grooved wheel inside a pulley – the piece that holds the rope or cable in place.

STOPE: An underground excavation along an ore body resulting from the mining of ore. Generally a large cavity/chamber extending up and down along the dip of the ore body as well as laterally along the length of the lode.

TIMBER SET: Constructed of a timber and lumber framework composed of horizontal wall plates and end plates and vertical posts used to support unstable ground.

TAILINGS: Waste rock that has gone through a mill and will be the size of sand or silt.

TRAMP MINER: A miner who moves from mine to mine and only works ten days to four months at each mine.

TRAMPIN' IN or OUT: Mining vernacular for hiring on at a mine or quitting work at a mine (both without much notice.)

WINDLASS: A simple hand-crank and reel mechanism used to raise ore or waste rock to the surface from a shaft or internal winze. Generally limited to prospecting with beginning shafts and small scale development work.

www.ingramcontent.com/pod-product-compliance
Lightning Source LLC
Chambersburg PA
CBHW061259110426
42742CB00012BA/1976